# PIXEL ESTATE

Just like your REAL ESTATE is your PLACE of doing business on earth, your PIXEL ESTATE is your PLACE of doing business on the internet.

And in today's day and age, the road to your REAL ESTATE goes through your PIXEL ESTATE.

Most businesses have well-appointed REAL ESTATE but may not have a well-appointed PIXEL ESTATE to match & mirror their identity.

Your PIXEL ESTATE is the FIRST thing your prospects and clients see before interacting with you.

**What are YOU willing to put YOUR NAME on?**

# For Dentists Only

A BUSINESS OWNER'S GUIDE TO
BUILDING WEB PAGES THAT SELL

# PIXEL ESTATE

How to Attract, Nurture, and Grow Leads by
Building Web Pages That Sell

PARTHIV
SHAH

Parthiv Shah., author

PIXEL ESTATE:
How to Attract, Nurture, and Grow Leads
by Building Web Pages That Sell / Parthiv Shah.

ISBN 9780990505952

# WELCOME AND THANK YOU!

Thank you for investing in a copy of my book. I appreciate your support and would like to give you access to a guide I created "Business Kamasutra, From Persuasion To Pleasure, The Art of Data and Business Relationships". This valuable guide gives you specific tactics to turn your business acquaintances into lifelong, prosperous relationships. It includes strategies on:

- Segmentation (chapter 3)
- Project planning (pages 42-56)
- Atomization (58-67)
- Outsourcing (page 74)
- Combining technology and training to grow your business (78-91)
- And much more!

### Click here to Access Business Kamasutra;

### https://www.businesskamasutra.com

# ALSO BY PARTHIV SHAH

❖ *The Iceberg You Don't See: The Marketing System for Financial Advisors*

❖ *Business Kamasutra: The Art of Data and Business Relations*

❖ *Business Kamasutra for Attorneys*

❖ *Business Kamasutra for Dentists*

❖ *Business Kamasutra for Pain Management Clinics*

❖ *"Ask": What Every Business Needs to Know About Making Money Predictably*

❖ *BRENT Never Forgets*

❖ *Secrets of the World's Most Potent & Persuasive Marketing Messages*

**A BUSINESS OWNER'S GUIDE TO SETTING UP INTEGRATED, AUTOMATED MARKETING**

# Forward:
## *Three Determainates Of Your Business' Success, Going Forward*
### by Dan S. Kennedy

From my 45+ years' in-trenches, hands-dirty experience turning small businesses into big and very big businesses through advertising and marketing, I ha three things to say about Parthiv Shah's book, chiefly focused on owning web pages i.e. internet real estate *that sells…*

**First, most of it *doesn't*.** Sad fact is, most landing pges, entire web sites, pages within the sites and attached funnels fail miserably at what, 90% of the time, should be their intended purpose; accountable results measured in dollars, not in views, minutes, likes or other new metrics nonsense. They fail because there is no "salesman" involved in their creation. They are hijacked by tech people and graphic artist and others who simply do not know how to sell and make real money from media, and worse, often, disdain the very idea of such harsh, "out-dated" accountability. You already know this, or at least know that the results from all that web site "stuff" you've done and keep doing isn't paying off, or you wouldn't be here. I'm just emphatically verifying what you know or, at least, feel in your gut. You are right.

It should be working better and doing more, and don't let anybody tell you different.

**Second, this has evolved into being damnably complicated – although that's why there is no much opportunity from getting it right, and into being vital for the very life of most businesses going forward.** I have lived long, and built businesses Before Internet, so I was around when having a web site was optional. Then they became, basically, online business cards. Now, they are part of a very complicated "pixel estate." It's the difference between a backyard garden still manageable with a hoe and a watering can, and a real working, modern farm, with main buildings, out-building, soil analysis and different prescribed fertilzers for different acres, automation, a multitude of equipment; a very *sophisticated* operation. And that is a key word: sophistication. I can now directly connect the degree of the sophistication of your pixel estate (design and engineering, data gathering and use, and accountability) with the size of your income, the growth possibility of your business, and its stability and security, especially in ever-more competitive and commoditizing markets.

You can no longer skate by with a "web designer" any more than you can get by with a business card designed for you at the local copy shop. Now you need an engineer, a designer, a top SALES copywriter, a data scientist and a results manager for a comprehensive pixel estate. Whether that is you, a current staff-person, a person hired for the jobs, or outsourced vendors, this book will honestly, candidly lay out ALL that is REQUIRED for success with your web site(s) and the different kinds of web pages that must comprise them.

Also, this is, in no way, optional or even of secondary importance anymore. If the China Virus' traumatizing of small businesses of every kind taught us anything, it is: andy and every business must be able to survive, even thrive *at its web sites*. If you want an ANTI-FRAGILE business, this is an imperative. It's okay, by the way, not to love this. I don't. But you don't dare let "not liking it" get in your way.

**Third and last, a Principle of mine: you get rich by what you OWN, not by what you DO.** Doing produces only income, most of which has a nasty habit of disappearing one way or another. OWNED ASSETS = EQUITY, which can provide wealth. The entire idea of having a Pixel Estate is Ownership, not (just) more Doing. The more sophistication baked into it, the more valuable it can be.

This author, Parthiv Shah, is an online marketing engineer, a designer, a data scientist and has a team of top sales copywriters, and is a results manager for comprehensive pixel estates. It's what he does. *All* he does. Yes, it's a little neardy. Might *not* be the guy you'd most enjoy watching a football game with at the bar. But *this* stuff, he knows inside out, upside down, 60 ways from Sunday. The "guts" of it all are the individual, inter-locked, sequential, different kinds of web pages, and he is neck deep in those guts every day. Also, importantly, he is the rare tech geek with a *salesman's* mind. You can trust what he presents in this book.

DAN S. KENNEDY

Serial entrepreneur, investor, strategic consultant, and author of 36 busienss books including the famous *NO B.S.* book series.

# CONTENTS

# PART 1

# WELCOME

## AN IMPORTANT NOTE

Every product has its brand—Starbucks has its expensive coffees, 7-11 has its Slurpee, and my brand is a helping business owners by giving them the information they need to grow their business. To that end, this book is the Coles Notes version of how to attract, nurture and convert your leads into customers by building web pages that sell.

# WHO SHOULD READ THIS BOOK?

No one knows more than I do how little time you have as an entrepreneur or business owner. That's why if my book is not for you, I don't want to waste what time you do have reading something that may not be relevant. That's why I'm going to be crystal clear about who can benefit from this short book.

I wrote this book for entrepreneurs and business owners who want to understand the components and phases of a Growth Driven Design (GDD) website (Pixel Estate) that sells. The acronyms and terms marketers and tech gurus throw around can confuse and frustrate the best of us, and I will define each of them before explaining how they work and why they are essential. Most of all, I want you to see how these sales and marketing techniques work and how they fit together within your GDD Pixel Estate.

This book is for local business owners, business executives, service people, and online entrepreneurs with one question in common. "How do I attract, capture, and build relationships with my potential customers that convert into lifelong revenue-producing relationships with my website?"

What I'm about to share in this book will show you a step by step process of how you can do precisely that.

If you can take the knowledge and expertise you have of your current customer relationships and apply it to the GDD system, which I will define a little later in this book; then I wrote this book for you.

This Book Is for The Person Who IS NOT Concerned About:

- Taking an honest look at where their website is succeeding and failing

- Admitting they may not have or even know what an effective website is, or, if they do have one, realize it is not working well

- Accepting information and feedback on what is working and what is not working with their current website

- Admitting they have little or limited knowledge of the anatomy of web pages that sell

- Confessing to a certain confusion over the thousands of pages of content telling you what does and does not sell on your website

- Acknowledging their website may be letting customers slip through the cracks

- Owning up to confusion over how the sales funnels work with their business system

- Accepting they have a lot to learn about attracting, maintaining, and wowing their new and existing customers with their website

- Disclosing their absence of knowledge over where customers are positioned on their sales pyramid

- Feeling a need for a website system that incorporates sales, marketing, and technological automation to free them up to focus on building their business rather than working in it

- Finding automation to free them up to focus on building their business rather than working in it

- This Book is for the Person Who IS Focused on:

- Applying an efficient system that quickly increases the speed of sales

- Adopting a system that automates and streamlines business processes and efficiencies

- Implementing marketing architecture that builds lifelong customer relationships

- Offering helpful content to prospects first and then connecting the dots to their products or services

- Enabling themselves to complete this book in about an hour

- Making money through nurturing prospects to take the next steps in their buyer's journey

- Leveraging technology to automate the majority of their sales funnel processes

- Leveraging data to make informed decisions about website refinement

- Learning how to turn leads into customers through a well-organized and planned buyer's journey

- Understanding the value of a GDD website for your Pixel Estate and business

- Realizing the potential of a GDD website for your Pixel Estate and business

Have no doubt; I'm going to share with you how you can achieve greater profits by integrating a GDD Pixel Estate with high conversion website pages that build lifelong customers.

If that sounds like something you'd like for your business, please keep reading.

# MY PROMISE
# TO YOU

If you're still reading this, book, I promise not to waste the next approximately one hour of your life. I sincerely hope this book gives you the information that helps you take the following steps to move your business forward.

Those who know me appreciate that I take my responsibility to the entrepreneurial community seriously and volunteer my time by helping fellow entrepreneurs with pro bono marketing consulting. They also know I am a respected teacher of marketing and e-business with a reputation for excellence backed by experience.

I promise to lend a hand to give you a proven and effective strategy for marketing with state-of-the-art technologies to execute your sales automation. Through automation, you will position yourself as the authority to build your know, like, and trust factor with your customers for your product or service. I'm going to tell you everything I know to make sure you have everything you need. In exchange, you need to try too. Take the responsibility to read this book and consider my information with an objective mindset.

In February 2002, when I left the J M Perrone Company to start ListLaunchers, we had a prayer ceremony at our new offices. Sitting on the floor, in front of my family, friends, and business associates, the priest said the following prayer. I still remember every word of it, as if it were yesterday:

"You have now embarked on a new journey by starting this business. For the next 1000 days, we the family, we the religion, we the society, relieve you of all your earthly responsibilities. Now, this is your place of work. This is your place of worship; this is your home, this is your playground. Sit down, get to work, and for the next 1000 days, commit your heart and soul to focus on making this work. At the end of 1000 days, you will be a successful businessman, a better family man, a better religious man, and a philanthropist who will be committed to making the world a better place!"

It is my heartfelt opinion what I'm about to share is:

- The most effective long-term way to connect with potential customers

- The most intelligent sales, marketing, and technology strategy to promote your business or service

- The fastest way for your business to build business success

- The simplest, most straightforward way to capture, nurture and develop leads into lifelong customers

Needless to say, if you need or want more details outside of what I was able to cover in this short book, you can reach out to me or access my other books, success blueprint, and CD by visiting http://www.elaunchers.com/library.

I want to start this book by saying this prayer for all my fellow entrepreneurs. May God bring you the same success he has brought to my family and me!

# INTRODUCTION

There are a few things I want to tell you about me before I start. Firstly, I've been in direct marketing since 1989. Secondly, I've been helping small to not-so-small businesses and organizations compete and win against rivals with huge marketing dollars. Thirdly, I have a bachelor's degree in sociology from Gujarat State University in India, and an MBA in marketing from Bentley University in Waltham, MA, USA. The reason the last point is important is because sociology is all about the study of relationships and institutions, and marketing is the activities we take to sell our products or services. They go together like peanut butter and jelly.

I published my first book, Business Kamasutra, From Persuasion to Pleasure, The Art of Data and Business Relations in 2015. Since 2002 I've been helping entrepreneurs and business owners build and automate their marketing campaigns by leveraging technology. I have a long and fruitful track record (19 years and counting) of supporting business owners in my community. My clients range from well-known, high-profile direct marketers to local dentists and chiropractors among many other professionals. We have mailed over a billion pieces of direct mail, produced over 10,000 marketing campaigns, built over 1000 websites and landing pages, and generated over 1,000,000 Personalised URL's (PURLS). It has been my privilege to have helped them. This is where my background in sociology comes into play. I love people, I love making friends, and I love helping people with their businesses. The longer I've been in business the more I realize three truths:

i.   Many books are buried in detail that overwhelm
     and confuse business owners and entrepreneurs

ii.  Although business owners start out with the best
     of intentions to read everything they can get their
     hands on about automated marketing processes, most
     books end up collecting dust on their bookshelves

iii. Entrepreneurs and business owners need
     brief, straightforward, information that gives
     them the basics in about an hour. They just
     don't have the bandwidth for anything else
     that's more involved or time consuming.

I'm always looking for ways to help people learn about systems that produce positive ROI for their integrated marketing campaigns. The result of this ongoing endeavor is my book, which focuses on automated lead capture, lead nurture, and relationship development. These things are important for your business because they convert your leads into lifelong customer relationships.

My book is geared towards 95% of business owners who want to solve the question I described earlier in "Who should read this book?"

My book is focused on three truths:

i.   It is designed as an overview of the complex and
     multi-faceted process of creating effective web pages.
     It is intended to be more like a GDD Website
     Development 101 rather than the entire encyclopedia.

ii.  Reading this book cover to cover will give you a
     sense of achievement that you now have a grasp
     of how create a GDD Pixel Estate that coverts.

iii. It helps everyday business owners and entrepreneurs
     to understand the processes and systems needed

to develop their own GDD Pixel Estate.

If you've ever wondered how to develop your web pages, but felt it was too complicated or time consuming, this short book is your recipe for success. Our excellence is powered by our experience.

Please know I will not be spending any time trying to persuade you that a GDD Pixel Estate is the way to go for website design. I assume, if you are reading this book, you've already convinced yourself and are looking for a breakdown of how the systems can work within your business.

So, grab a coffee, find a comfortable chair, put on your reading glasses, and let me walk you through the journey. If you have any questions or comments, please book time with me at www.meetparthiv.com.

In gratitude

*Parthiv*

P.S.: When you've finished reading this book would you please leave a truthful Amazon book review? Reviews are a great way to help others solve the same problem, and I respond to all reviews, and appreciate your feedback.

## REMEMBER TO GET THIS!

If you haven't already grabbed your copy, make sure you download my "Success Blueprint For Growth" at www.parthivfreereport.com. Remember, A CEO does only THREE things: Revenue Economics, Marketing Plan and Marketing Budget. This blueprint guides you through the process of articulating your revenue economics and develop your marketing activities & budget for year and quarter. Again the link is **www.parthivfreereport.com**

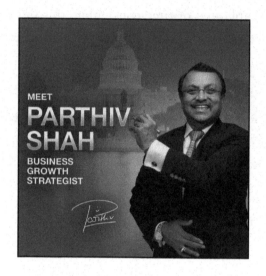

Book time with Parthiv at
www.meetparthiv.com
and claim your gifts.

# PART 2

# Growth Driven Design Blueprint for Your Pixel Estate

"

# Great design is the difference between lackluster and outstanding results

**PARTHIV SHAH**

# CHAPTER 1
# YOUR PIXEL ESTATE

The internet has become as real a place to us as our bricks-and-mortar homes or businesses. I call the internet the "Place Estate." In fact, many spend more time on their Place Estate than they do at home. Although many companies have both a physical business and a website, many businesses no longer have storefronts. Their website or even their Facebook page is their primary place of business. I call this the "Pixel Estate." In today's market, your Pixel Estate is more critical than your Place Estate, and in reality, it determines the success or failure of your business.

The old school "launch and leave" cookie-cutter website has become a thing of the past. Your Pixel Estate is the first place your customers visit, and in some cases (especially during COVID), the only place customers visit. Your website, blog, funnels, and micro-sites, as well as your print assets, comprise your entire Pixel Estate. "Nearly 21.55% of the World's population buy online. In 2021, the number is expected to rise to over 2.14 billion." Therefore, your pixel estate must be designed and executed to appeal to your customer's needs and wants, reduce any apprehensions, and guide them through the buyer's journey. It must be visually, structurally, and functionally sound to convert prospects into sales.

## Growth-Driven Design Pixel Estates

The "launch and leave" websites of the past took months to build, were over budget, expensive and inefficient. Luckily, they are phasing out in favor of a more agile approach focused on optimization results and data-driven design. This new Pixel Estate website is referred to as Growth-Driven Design or a GDD website. Learn more about this concept at www.growthdrivendesign.com

With a GDD website, your Pixel Estate launches quickly, the investment is spread out over time, and the website continually changes and improves month-to-month. Changes occur based on data-driven results and decisions. A GDD Pixel Estate captures your values and personality so that your audience grows to know, like, and trust you and your product/service.

With a GDD Pixel Estate, you can see which parts of your website generate the most business and put your efforts into maximizing those targeted areas. Over time, and with your Pixel Estate's data, you will understand your customer's needs and wants, which will support you in creating your individualized buyer's journey. With A GDD Pixel Estate, the customer's data is based on their needs and wants. It shapes your content, products, and buyer's journey. Content from traditional static websites is based on assumptions and follows a "hit and miss" strategy. Because a GDD website is based on customer data, it eliminates the guesswork, targeting content/products to your customers needs/wants.

## The Role of Data in your Pixel Estate

The backbone of your Pixel Estate is where your data lives and is also called your data warehouse or data cube. Picture your data cube as a gated environment, where your prospects and clients enter under constant surveillance. It stores and tracks information 24/7 and provides you with data that shapes how your GDD Pixel Estate evolves and changes over time. Customer data can be divided into three areas, the data cube, the data pyramid, and the data prism.

## Data Cube

Within your GDD Pixel Estate, your tools, techniques, and pre-built collection of technologies work in tandem to choreograph pixel, paper, plastic, and phone communications for an effective sales conversion platform.

Your data cube includes your prospects, clients, and influencers. Because they interact with your technology asynchronously, it is called a "touchless sales environment." Your data cube consists of sophisticated technology that connects your website, blog, landing pages, and sales funnels to your Customer Relationship Management to automate the sales/marketing process. Touchless technology seamlessly choreographs your user experience from welcoming, dispensing personalized content to nurturing, indoctrinating, and monitoring their consumption. Once the customer data assimilates, they know, like, and trust you and are ready for their first conversation with your sales team or placed in your automated nurture program.

## Data Pyramid

Not all customer relationships are created equally. Some are more valuable than others. The pyramid spectrum identifies and segregates customers by assigning a value. Once you know where your customer lands on the pyramid spectrum, you can determine how much energy you want to put into that relationship. This method concentrates your efforts on the customers who are most valuable to you and eliminates everyone else.

## Data Prism

Now that you know who should be on which level of your money pyramid, you can create the processes that place your customers on specific pyramid spectrums. Just as a prism takes white light and separates it into a prism/rainbow of colors, a data prism takes universal data and slices it into segments. Individual segments give you knowledge of who, when, where, and what to focus your marketing energy on for the most profitable results.

## The GDD Strategy

The Growth-Driven Design journey follows a three-phase process that supports a lean, efficient approach to minimizing time and costs, and maximizing optimization and includes; strategy, launch pad, and continuous improvement.

The strategy phase involves seven key steps.

**Key 1**  Reach consensus with all stakeholders on the value of a GDD website before starting

**Key 2**  Website Waterfall Workflow — create efficiency and minimize costs by following the five-step waterfall process.

    i.   Create strategy first before the design

    ii.  Craft a page prototype before the design

    iii. Design the prototype

    iv. Finalize the website in Hubspot and Launch

    v.  Generate a wish list

**Key 3** Time each Phase — traditional websites have indefinite timelines and budgets. With a GDD website, each phase of the website divides into "boxed-sprints" which translates into two-week time blocks.

**Key 4** Launch the two key pages first. Based on the Pareto principle, 80% of your results come from 20% of your work; with GDD, focus your efforts on launching two key pages, then add lower priority pages at later dates.

**Key 5** Insert your analytics and metrics, including heatmap, screen remodeling, Pingdom, BrowserTest.com, Page Performance Tool, and all redirects, links, etc. needed for a smooth launch.

**Key 6** Host a stakeholder review and make final amendments, report bugs, add notations to analytics and refresh heatmaps, schedule post-launch review, and prioritize a Wishlist one week before launch.

**Key 7** Implement five supportive communication techniques

    i.   Track all requests through a single help-desk email

    ii.  Add stakeholders to a collaboration channel like Slack or Hipchat

    iii. Gather all feedback internally and provide an aggregated report rather than numerous conflicting responses

    iv. Set up once a week "office hours" to propel the launch momentum

    v.  Deal with the boxed sprints first, and park all other discussions for later dates

By applying the waterfall-style stages, you can completely avoid delays, revisions, and endless stalls.

## The GDD Launch

Before hammering in the first nail of your GDD Pixel Estate, build your foundation with specific, measurable, achievable, results-focused, and timed (SMART) objectives. Next, collect and prioritize your ideas. Actions can then grow out of objectives with sprints, monthly, or quarterly timed goals while applying the waterfall five-step process.

## GDD Continuous Improvement

Optimal performance can only be achieved by tracking results and making "many small refinements over time." A GDD Pixel Estate requires continuous improvement.

A GDD Pixel Estate is agile, low-risk, and refined. A static "launch and leave" website is frustrating to develop and redevelop, expensive, is disconnected to data-driven resultand has boundless timelines. In contrast, your GDD website is a living, breathing organism that provides continuous feedback that supports optimization of your Pixel Estate within a constantly evolving Place Estate. I have written this book to support you in building your Pixel Estate and eventually your Pixel Empire.

**To find out more about how GDD works, scan the QR code below, or click the link.**

**https://growthdrivendesign.com/**

# CHAPTER 2
# WHAT IS WEB PAGE OPTIMIZATION AND WHY YOU SHOULD OPTIMIZE YOUR WEB PAGES?

You may have already discovered that most websites (what I call "Pixel Estates"), typically have five key web pages that sell:

I. Cold Page

II. Warm Page

III. Hot Page

IV. Lead Magnet Page

V. Offer Page

VI. Home

In an ideal world, each page of your website works towards maximizing your desired business results and also fits with your overall marketing strategy. Website pages that maximize your business results are called "optimized" pages or "web pages that sell".

To figure out how to optimize each of these pages, you'll need to answer two basic questions first:

1. What does the user want? Or, what problem or issue drove them to look for a solution on your website? Or, what information are they seeking as a solution to their problem?

2. How can you give them the information they need so that you can ask them to do something you want?

To answer the first question, its helpful to know where they were before they found your website. Did they visit your site because you sent them an email? Did they run a Google search? Once you know what they want and where the came from, you can deliver the information they want in an easily digestible format such as a video, diagram, or report.

To answer the second question, you need to put a clear, direct, call to action (CTA) on each and every one of your web pages. If you think of your website as a bricks and mortar store, wouldn't it make sense to have every customer who enters your store buy something? If you answered yes, then you want a warm or hot page rather than a cold page. If optimizing your webpages is beginning to sound interesting, keep reading, because this book is for you.

An excellent example of an optimized, well laid out Home Page is my client Dr. Vinton's website https://www.drkenvinton.com/. Patients from all over the world seek him out for relief from debilitating pain —without medication.

Who is looking for him? People who want long-term relief from pain without mediation. How are they finding him? Googling "pain relief".

His website has three tabs at the top that focus on the two reasons people end up on his website; problem with pain management and how to get relief from pain immediately. He also addresses any resistance to his method with the "Why The Vinton Method?" tab.

He does a very skillful job of getting into his patient's heads to address the question of why prior treatments with other systems haven't worked. He answers that question right away with another optimized button that links to the explanation.

What does he want his potential patients to do? "Get Started" and "Get Relief Today". This is done with three CTA buttons on his Home Page. An obvious CTA button in the upper right-hand corner, a second CTA button beside the "why most treatments fail", followed by testimonials and a third CTA "Get Relief Today" button at the bottom of the page.

Although Dr. Vinton doesn't have an "About Page" he has a "Why the Vinton Method" tab at the top, which serves the same purpose. His potential patients want information about the treatment method, and how it works, and want proof of the miraculous results he's achieved. Note this page aims it's focus on what the patient wants and needs. Dr. Vinton provides answers to patient questions with short videos from actual patients. On this page he has six (yes six!) CTA's that prompt the user to:

1. "Get Started"

2. "Discover Which Pain You May Have"

3. Encourage action with, "I'm Ready for Relief"

4. Create urgency, "I'm Ready for Relief Today"

5. "Get Relief"

This is a great example of an "About" page that drives optimization. Is it about the company? Yes, in that it describes the treatments, but it's primarily focused on the user and the value they can get from treatments with Dr. Vinton.

Let's look at the optimization techniques that are used on each of his pages:

1.  He has a HUGE headline that zeros in on his patient's problems directly and clearly

2.  He has a logical flow of information, addressing the patient's issues, and telling them exactly what to do next with his CTA's

3.  His CTA's are obvious, direct, and impossible to miss

4.  His most important information is in the top portion of the web page (top fold)

5.  He includes many CTA's on each page

6.  His CTA's allow his patients to contact him easily to schedule an appointment

7.  His website focuses on the problem his patients have and the immediate resolution of their pain—without medication

In short, an optimized page knows what users want, delivers exactly that, and asks them to act in return. Your website needs to provide users with knowledge that demands a response. Give them what they want. Then ask for what you want. Your website is not a place to play coy.

In the subsequent chapters I'll teach you step by step what to include and how to optimize your results so that your website becomes a lean, mean, money-making machine.

# CHAPTER 3
# FIVE KEY PAGES THAT SELL

*"Today is not about get the traffic, its about get the targeted and relevant traffic."*

— Steve Audette

In a profitable website, there are really only five pages that sell, the cold page, the warm page, the hot page, the home page, and the landing page. I'll be sharing everything I know about each page in the next few chapters, so buckle up!

## I. The Cold Page

My best friend Tom's first management job was in a large community college administering corporate education programs. He thought he had a pretty solid understanding of the function and duties of the role from the job description and interviews.

Four months into the job, he got a call from one of his major clients asking why they hadn't received an invoice? Up until that point, Tom had no idea invoicing or budgeting for his corporate training management role as part of the job. So, he jumped in and created a bunch of invoices, only to have one of his colleagues ask, " what are you doing?!" Apparently, his part of the invoicing process involved generating PO's and submitting them to the payroll department. As it turned out, invoicing was the tip of the iceberg. Budgeting and quarterly financial forecasting were tasks he had to perform in his management capacity.

He had no idea.

Tom had never worked in management for a large educational institution and was completely unaware of the budgeting/financial process. He didn't know there was a problem with his lack of budgeting skills because he didn't think he was responsible for budgeting. He didn't know what he didn't know. Tom was problem unaware and solution unaware.

## Problem and Solution Unaware

Think of your cold page as a place where people land searching for information. It's your job to take problems they are unaware of and make them aware of the pain points or consequences. Until you have shown them a potential pain point, they won't know whether they want your product or service. Your cold page needs to show them the pain points and how your product or service solves or resolves their pain points or needs, and while this is happening, you need to establish trust and credibility. Bear in mind that they don't know you, your product, or your service, and will most likely be wondering why they should trust you or even welcome your advice.

## The Difference between A Lead and A Prospect

At this point, it's essential to differentiate between a prospect and a lead. Potential customers who have visited your page or blog or have provided their contact information in exchange for a free report or whitepaper are leads. A prospect is interested in your product/service and is your ideal customer.

Back to my friend Tom, when he started his position, he was problem and solution unaware. He might have been looking through websites for ideas about popular corporate training programs and chanced across information about budgeting. He may have considered it good advice to have down the road and moved on. This action made him a lead. Once he realizes his position involves intricate knowledge of budgeting procedures that he lacks, he becomes problem aware and solution unaware.

He then targets his search on websites that offer budgeting training. He is shopping for information that will bridge his knowledge gap and download information that introduces him to budgeting training programs. This action makes him a prospect.

Both leads and prospects require nurturing until they buy your product or service.

## Creating Evaluation Criteria

Researching who is the best fit and the likelihood of them buying will determine whether you have a prospect or a lead. You can do this by developing a set of evaluation criteria and keeping records of your potential and existing customers and where they are in the sales cycle. Most businesses call this their customer relationship management or CRM. CRM's can start with excel spreadsheets; however, once your customer base grows, an investment in CRM software can help keep you sane.

Using Tom as the budgeting software company's ideal client, prospecting criteria would include:

- upper management

- in positions that pay 100K/year or more

- working at for-profit departments in educational institutions or corporate training departments in the profit industry

- require detailed budget information online

- sophisticated digital skills

- level of education — master's degree or higher

- budget of $1500-$2000 per training program

Tom is at the problem and solution unaware stage and has landed on your cold page accidentally. Tom landed on your cold page because he was looking for popular corporate training and noticed your website since he will be doing budgeting. Tom doesn't know what budgeting involves or how much of it he will have to complete at this stage. He also has no idea if he can complete this task with his current knowledge or if he requires additional training.

## Moving from a Cold page to a Warm Page

Tom's actions or inactions determine where you can move him within your sales process. If Tom downloads website information on budgeting software, he becomes a lead. Once he realizes he needs knowledge of budgeting procedures, he becomes problem aware and solution unaware. At that point, he will seek out specific websites for products/services that give him information about his situation.

Once Tom downloads free information such as a report or whitepaper, he moves from a lead to a prospect. Now he is ready to move to your warm page.

## II. The Warm Page

Following along Tom's budgeting journey… at the end of his fourth month of work in the corporate training department, his manager gives him a copy of the previous quarter's detailed budget report. It's accompanied with links to spreadsheets. His manager gives it to him well ahead of his budget forecast deadline. Tom reads through it and is so confused he can't even formulate a question. Tom knows he has a problem but isn't sure what to do. Tom is at the problem aware and solution unaware stage.

Tom starts his search on the internet and targets three budgeting software companies and offers up his contact information in exchange for downloadable reports. Tom's actions have flagged him as interested and made him a "warm" prospect.

## Inbound and Outbound Marketing

Many websites create opportunities for both inbound and outbound marketing. With inbound marketing, a potential customer contacts you about your product/service. With outbound marketing you contact a potential customer about your product/service. Outbound marketing leads the way for most businesses with 74% of companies using inbound over outbound marketing. An effective approach though, is to do both.

Once you have a warm prospect—what can you do to nurture your prospects along the buyer's journey with inbound marketing?

- Create a segmented email campaign that only shares relevant information. The content should identify the pain points and create openings for conversation

- Track your website visitor analytics and collect email addresses for those who have viewed or downloaded multiple information

- Create lead magnets that are available as downloads on

your website in exchange for names/email addresses

- Connect with people or companies on social media such as LinkedIn who appear to be a good fit for your product/service

- Ask for referrals from your current customers, or create a referral program that rewards customers for referrals

Throughout the inbound process you have been sending "Tom" information that helps solve the problem. Now you're ready to reach out and have a conversation with him to gain a deeper understanding of who he is and what he needs. This is the often-dreaded follow-up or discovery call.

Understand Tom may or may not be a fit for your product (people change jobs and don't always update their LinkedIn profiles) and if not, refer him to another reliable source. Offering help regardless of whether you get the sale is good karma, and I guarantee, it always comes back to you.

## The Discovery Call

During the conversation ask Tom qualifying questions:

- Is the product in Tom's industry?

- Does Tom have familiarity with the products/services

- Or specifically for Tom, does the budgeting software training focus on for profit corporate training departments?

- If so, is Tom the person who is buying it or is someone else making the buying decision?

- Is Tom's purchase a one-off or is there potential to offer Tom lifetime value?

- Is Tom a decision-maker at work or an influencer? In Tom's case he could be both. He is buying this product for his personal use. However, once he uses it and experiences success, he may become a raving fan. As a raving fan he may suggest that the entire department buy the software to achieve consistent budgeting standards. In the future, Tom could create a compelling case to decision-makers on your behalf.

- Is anyone else involved in deciding whether to buy this product? For example, Tom may consult with his wife or work manager before buying.

- Does this purchase come out of his direct budget?

Throughout the discovery process, your goal is to identify Tom's pain points and to identify any challenges he has that stop him from buying the product.

## Answering Objections

Time and money usually present the biggest objections, and this is why it's important to have the answers to the objections ready. For example, Tom's objections could include; why buy this training program and what makes this program better than the others?

It's good practice to sift out the buyers who are qualified to buy your product now vs. those who either do not have the time or money and should be revisited later. Doing this will save you and the buyer time.

## Converting Warm to Hot Pages

Once you have assessed Tom's challenges, and pain points it's time to covert him into a customer by showing him the value he'll get from buying your product. During the close, which happens in the hot phase, there are really only two predictable outcomes; sale won (Tom buys your product) or sale lost (Tom doesn't buy your product). Also called a closing ratio.

Regardless of the outcome, researching your prospect is ongoing. Looking at prospect's websites, LinkedIn Profiles, and social media channels keep you in the loop as to whether they are a qualified prospect, and how you can target your follow up communication to their specific goals. No one pays attention to generic emails for the masses, people want the human touch.

Tom is at the problem aware and solution unaware stage, and with your skilled inbound process, is ready to move to your hot page.

## III. The Hot Page

Tom gets word from his manager that the budget reports are due in three weeks. He doesn't want to wait any longer. He needs to decide on the software program he'll buy and learn the information quickly so he can get the job done. Tom has downloaded free reports and information from free sites and has shortlisted three products. Tom is ready for the hot page.

A hot page should do several things; identify the problem, agitate the issue, discredit the solution, and solve the problem. The marketing acronym for this strategy is called PADS.

### Identify the problem

Prospects need to know that you have a deep understanding of their problem. You can demonstrate this by identifying some of their major pain points.

- Does Tom need to understand the budgeting jargon so

that he can decipher the instructions for the report?

- Is Tom worried that not being able to complete
  the report correctly could get him fired?

- Is Tom worried he could miss the point of
  the report because of his inexperience?

You need to get inside Tom's head and figure out what's keeping him up nights and creating a knot in his stomach during the day when he talks to his manager.

## Agitate the problem

You've already identified the problem/problems; now you need to keep poking at them so that Tom knows you understand what's really bothering him.

Dig deeper to find the source of the emotional wound and pour a little lemon juice on it. Then share the consequences of not solving the problem.

- Are you worried your knowledge of budgets is
  so limited you'll embarrass yourself by not even
  being able to figure out the instructions?

- Do you toss and turn at night worrying that your boss will
  expose your lack of critical budgeting knowledge and fire you?

- Does the thought of scheduling a meeting with your
  manager to go over your budget report twist your stomach
  in knots because you're afraid of being exposed as a fraud?

- Are you afraid that you are weakest link of the
  chain in your department because you don't have
  a clue how to complete a budget forecast?

Agitating the problem gets your prospect's attention and creates an impact by drawing a picture of worst-case scenarios.

## Discredit Typical "Alternate" Solutions

You've been dripping lemon juice into the emotional wound and now that your prospect can see it bleeding you are going to add a dash of salt by discrediting typical solutions.

For example, the hard truth about choosing to skip training and learn the skills on the job from colleagues — is that doesn't work. Poor Tom might align himself with a colleague who isn't good at budgeting but thinks he is a wizard. Tom could end up ingraining mistakes and making an even bigger mess of his first attempt at budgeting than he anticipated. The other issue is that he must wait until someone has time to teach him, in-between getting their own work done. His training may never happen, and his budget may not be completed. There is also the risk that his colleague might expose him to the manager, which could get him fired. Or that he might owe the colleague for their efforts and for covering up his lack of knowledge. All these scenarios make him queasy.

Then, after you strike down each of Tom's obvious but futile options, you can offer your solution.

In the discredit phase, you're taking Tom to a place where his future is bleak. "You could wait for a colleague to show you what they know about budgeting when they can fit you in if they can fit you in. Or you can hope and pray that the person who offers help actually knows what they're doing. You can hope that they keep your secret to themselves rather than sharing it with the manager…"

## Solve the Problem

Now, for the icing on the cake—show your solution by answering each of their questions/pain points.

"Or you could fast track your budgeting knowledge with our step-by-step online training created by chartered accountants who have over 25 years of specialized knowledge of the corporate training world."

- Your manager put her trust in you. Don't let her down with gaps in budgeting information and incomplete reporting. Our budgeting software is created by chartered accountants who have over 25 years of specialised knowledge of the corporate training arena. ZZZ Budgeting software walks you through a step-by-step accredited process to build your understanding the right way from the foundation up.

- Secure your future by learning skills and knowledge you can pick up in the security of your own home within a time frame that works with your schedule. ZZZ Budgeting Software turbo-charges you through the essentials while providing the tools necessary to excel as a professional budget manager.

- Provide valuable financial insights to your team and managers with ZZZ Budgeting Software through our comprehensive budget analysis tracking system.

Tom gets the chance to fill in his knowledge gaps with a legit program created by professionals who understand budgeting and his specific work niche. He is reassured it can happen in the comfort of his own home and on his own schedule. ZZZ Budgeting Software saves Tom the embarrassment of having his knowledge gaps exposed and presents him as a polished professional who can add valuable insights to the department.

The hot webpage with its problem, agitate, discredit, solution (PADS) strategy creates empathy with your prospect. The PADS system activates two primal human emotions; pleasure and pain, with pain being the stronger motivator.

Your hot page is compelling because it hammers home the pain and soothes with your pleasurable solution.

## IV. The Lead Magnet Page/AKA Home Page

"75% of consumers admit to making judgements on a company's credibility based on the company's website design." (Source. SWEOR.com, 2020)

Your lead magnet/home page is a critical business tool that acts as your business's first impression. An in-person first impression takes 7 seconds. Your home page only has 3 seconds to make an excellent first impression. In those 3 seconds, your homepage must introduce your product/service and compel visitors to explore your site or download your resource/s. Your homepage is the lead magnet that sets the stage for initiating conversations and generating leads.

An effective home page is divided into 14 key content features that are vital to its success.

### 1. Logo and Headline

*Did you know...*

"It takes 2.6 seconds for a user's eyes to land on the area of a website that most influences their first impression. Users spend an average of 5.94 seconds looking at a website's main image. The same study found 46% of consumers based their decisions on the credibility of the websites on their visual appeal and aesthetics." (Source. SWEOR. com, 2020).

A picture paints a thousand words, and for branding to make an impact, it should be front and center on the top of your website and link to your homepage. Aim for a clear, simple headline that allows your target audience to understand exactly what your product/service does within seconds

## 2. Sub-headline

*Did you know…*
"Users spend an average of 5.59 seconds looking at a website's written content."

"70% of small business websites lack a CTA on their homepage". (Source. SWEOR.com, 2020)

Your sub-headline should complement your headline and provide a brief description of what you offer while targeting a pain point that your product/service resolves.

## 3. Calls to Action or CTA's

You want your visitors to buy your product/service, and your CTA's above the fold exist to direct people to different stages of your buying funnel. Link your CTA's to landing pages, contact forms, enrollment forms, or any other website pages that give the visitor more information. Do make sure that you; include an obvious visual image for your CTA, have plenty of white space around your CTA so that visitors only click on the CTA, and that the CTA's are short (less than five words) and highly action-oriented.

## 4. Image or Video

*Did you know…*

Two thirds of people would rather read something beautifully designed than something plain." (Source. SWEOR.com, 2020)

An image or video of your product/service can get your message across quickly and simply while adding interest and emotion to your page. High-quality images that capture feeling add integrity and believability to your website.

## 5. Benefits

You might think the benefits of buying your product/service are apparent, but prospects need to know the impact your product/service has on the users to understand the advantages in a conversational tone. Visitors want easy-to-read content that sounds the same as conversational language. Gone are the days of formal writing and wordy explanations.

## 6. Proof

It's human nature to want to see what other people are doing, how they do it, and how they benefited before buying it yourself. Testimonials carry more weight coming from satisfied customers than from your business. They inspire trust and identify user insights. Be sure to include real testimonials with first and last names/images to show your audience they are legit.

## 7. Navigation Route

*Did you know…*

"First impressions are 94% design-related, which means if your website is too complicated, busy, and navigation is difficult to find—you'll lose most of your audience."

Do you like spending your time searching for information? Neither do your visitors. Have a clear navigation route visible on top of your page to make it easy and quick for customers to find what they are seeking.

## 8. Content Offer

Gifting excellent free resources such as whitepapers, eBooks, cheat sheets, webinars, or guides, demonstrates your knowledge and credibility to prospects and encourages them along the buyer's path by helping them solve their problem.

## 9. Secondary CTA's

Not everyone will be interested in your primary CTA, so it's a good idea to include secondary CTA's to capture additional prospects. These CTA's can be included below the fold.

## 10. List features

A feature is a part of your product or service, such as Tesla's automatically opening and closing doors and adjustable trunk sizes. You know your product or service better than anyone. Make sure you tell your audience everything about it in a concise and easy-to-read style.

## 11. Resources

Free resources are a great method of keeping visitors on your site longer and establishing your trustworthiness as an expert.

## 12. Awards and recognitions

Have you won industry awards or special honors? It is your time to legitimately brag about your accomplishments and demonstrate your standing as an industry expert on this page.

## 13. Optimized for mobile devices

### *Did you know...*

"57% of internet users won't recommend a business with a poorly designed website on mobile."

"Smartphones held a 63% share of all retail website visits.

Eight out of 10 customers would stop engaging with content that doesn't display well on their device, and 40% will visit a competitor's site instead." (Source: SWOR.com, 2020)

With most impulse buying taking place on cell phones, wouldn't it make good sense to ensure your website is optimized for both pc's and mobile devices?

## 14. Informational Footer

Once your visitor has reached the bottom of your page, they will want one or all of three things: your contact information, links to interior pages, or links to social media. The way people like to receive, and digest information varies, and social media is a great method of giving visitors another way to engage and connect with your/your business and to see social proof of your credibility.

## The Lead Magnet Sales Trail

A lead magnet is a marketing tool that helps you gain a prospect's contact data in exchange for information that helps them solve or at the very least — understand their problem. A good lead magnet will attract prospects to your website and when they choose to download your information, it generates leads. Thus, the name lead magnet. A lead magnet can take all types of forms from videos, podcasts, eBooks, whitepapers, courses, templates, and contests, to formulas that calculate interest rates, to virtually anything else downloadable.

When a prospect clicks a call to action, CTA button it takes them to a landing page, which is a standalone web page on your website, created to market a single focus or goal. On the landing page, prospects can download free information or buy a product/service. A landing page only has one goal, to sell one product/service. That singular goal makes your landing page a hard-working conversion generator that reduces time and cost of gaining a sales lead. Your landing page is the 5th page that sells.

There are basically two types of landing pages:

- Lead producing landing pages, which use a form that collects names and emails as their CTA

- Clickthrough landing pages, these have clickthrough pages that drive the prospect straight to the sales or subscription

To understand where landing pages fit within the scheme of your Pixel Estate, it is necessary to understand the steps in the sales trail.

## The Sales Trail

Having a killer lead magnet alone isn't enough. The lead magnet needs to follow a step-by-step sales conversion trail starting with a Call to Action or CTA.

## The Call to Action (CTA)

Prospects typically seek out your website because they are looking for specific products or services or information on products or services. To capture a prospect's contact information, you need to have a compelling CTA. A CTA is a button that takes the prospect to your landing page where they enter their information in exchange for a download to your lead magnet.

## The Landing Page

The landing page is where the prospect enters their contact information. It can be very simple such as a three-line form asking for a name and email address or a full-on sales page that follows the Pain, Agitate, Solve, Discredit, Solve (PADS) system and offers up testimonials from happy customers.

## The Thank You Page

After prospects have entered their information, they receive a download and a thank you page that informs prospects they have been added to your list. For most sales trails, that's the end of the process.

## Follow-up Email

For those with a clever behind-the-scenes programmer who understands relationship building or who have signed up for a CRM system such as HubSpot, there's one more step. The follow-up email sends a continuation message to your lead which starts a conversation.

If you have heaps of time on your hands to create lead magnets—you fall under the mythical and rare category of a "unicorn" business owner. The rest of us business owners, learn to maximize our time by using current resources or finding creative ways to repurpose resources into irresistible lead magnets. Here are some ideas for how to get maximum mileage from your content.

## How To Get Maximum Mileage

## From Your Blog Posts

Blog posts are the potatoes and rice of your meal. They can be served up alone as a dish or spiced up and added to new dinners or reconfigured for an entirely different meal. Blog posts, too, can be repurposed into many types of lead magnets, and each should include a content specific CTA. Here are 19 ideas to get you started, and some examples of content specific CTAs;

1.  eBooks compiled from a series of blog posts about a related subject all bundled into one convenient package. You can create an e-book from any series of articles on an associated topic or theme.

    *Example CTAs: Get my free eBook, download my book now, I want to read this eBook, Download the free guide, Unlock the power of this guide, send my free eBook!*

2.  Guest blog books are assembled from blogs written for posts other than your website. Although Google doesn't allow you to publish the same article on two different sites, a guest blog eBook is allowable.

    *Example CTAs: Learn how to do .....by ....
    In ....days. click here, Want to know what we know? Click here, Like what you're reading?
    Click here, get the complete guide to ....*

3.  An ultimate guide or roundup is a comprehensive collection of the best articles about a specific subject. A roundup is a great in-depth resource that streamlines information into a short easy to digest format.

    *Example CTAs: Free exclusive ...tips, sign up now! Want to be part of our community? Join us!, Ready to take control of your ...? Get Started!*

4.  A bonus offer is an addition to an existing package.

If you have a package of 10 items and have an article, form, etc., that would nicely compliment, add it in.

***Example CTAs:*** *Yes! Give me the bonus now! I want to learn for free + get a bonus!*

5.  A how-to guide from a tactical blog post offers help on any subject area. People constantly search the internet to figure out how to do something, how-to articles are always popular.

    ***Example CTAs:*** *Signup to jump start your education on ...! Learn More about how to..., Get your free ... guide, Learn how to....Fast track your learning now!*

6.  Blogs can be easily repurposed into a checklist. Checklists are a well-loved format that gives readers/skimmers the Coles notes version of a topic.

    ***Example CTAs:*** *Download my checklist now! Send it! Give me the short version now!*

7.  Blogs, interviews or podcasts can be turned into a workbook. Workbooks apply your strategies to specific issues in a logical sequence. Workbooks are helpful for the user, and they showcase you as an expert by teaching readers how to apply concepts to their reality.

    ***Example CTAs:*** *Let's get you started, It's-too-good-to-be-free, Download my workbook, Claim your workbook, Get started!*

8.  Regenerate your blog into a case study that defines the problem the customer entered with and the statistics for the solution's success. Everyone loves a story, and case studies are definitely a lot more interesting than a pile of statistics.

*Example CTAs: I want to learn more, Send me some insight, Show me real solutions to real problems.*

9. Would you like to hear a secret? Got your attention—didn't I? You can do the same with this tactic by remodeling an insight into an insider industry secret.

   *Example CTAs: Want in on the secret? Shhh, click here, Be very quiet, while clicking here*

10. Cheat sheets are not only helpful to your reader but serve as a great marketing tool for you as they are often shared or used as an industry reference guide.

    *Example CTAs: Show me how, Send my cheat sheet, Give me a short-cut!*

11. Webinar's are an excellent opportunity to showcase a subject where you have expertise and insight. It's easy to convert a blog into a short, entertaining webinar.

    *Example CTAs: Let me learn for free, Explore, Yes! I want to experience change! Book my webinar*

12. Infographics provide a healthy break from words, words, and yet more words. They can also get the point across in seconds. Let your creative juices flow when transforming your idea into an inforgraphic.

    *Example CTAs: Explore, Discover, Show me, Paint a picture*

13. Your customers buy your product, yes, but they'll stay with you for your personality and values. Personal stories are a fantastic way for your audience to get to know you.

    *Example CTAs: I'd like to hear more, Send me the scoop, Go ahead, make my day, share*

14. Develop your blog into a short eCourse. A course is a variation on the webinar theme, and highlights your expertise, knowledge, and builds credibility.

    ***Example CTAs:*** *Try this course for free, Discover new ideas, Yes! I want to learn for free, Book my e-course now!*

15. An Interview, podcast, or video is an excellent method of sharing information and gaining trust and credibility. Interviews or interview articles work well when you don't have a lot of time but have some excellent industry contacts who can share their knowledge with your audience.

    ***Example CTAs:*** *Watch video, Get a leg up in seconds, Take a tour*

16. Offer a newsletter. Your newsletter provides subscribers with your latest and greatest content in your niche area. You can also insert CTA's in your blog posts so that readers can subscribe directly to your newsletter/blog.

    ***Example CTAs:*** *Unlock wisdom, save my seat, Get instant access to .....newsletter! Become a ...., Yes, sign me up! Yes! I want in, I'm in*

17. A great way to attract new visitors/leads is to create an event. Fashion your event out of your most popular blog posts with guest speakers who can link your landing page to their individual landing pages.

    ***Example CTAs:*** *I'm coming! Join us! I'll give your....event a try*

18. Try before you buy is a long-standing method of attracting and retaining customers. Gifting a free trial of a product/service is an excellent conversation opener.

> **Example CTAs:** *Send me specials now!*
> *Claim your free…, Receive the magic*

19. Invitation-only pages/groups foster a feeling of belong, trust and exclusivity. Many businesses have private community groups such as FaceBook. Invite visitors to join your community.

   > **Example CTAs:** *Yes, I want to be included! Yes, take me there, Be part of the community*

Aren't you glad you don't have to start from scratch to create lead magnets? You've already written the content in your blog posts. All that's left is to modify your content into irresistible lead magnets and include content specific CTAs. Soon you'll be attracting your customers into your customer contact database and leading them through the buyer's journey.

## V. The Offer Page/AKA the Landing Page

Offer pages are known by many names including landing page, lead capture page, single property page, static page, squeeze page, or destination page. Those monikers are simply used to describe a page on your website that displays sales copy directed at one product/ service. An offer page can exist as its own micro website or can be a single page within a website.

Does it affect your ROI?

A better question, is how does it affect your ROI? If you have a website without an offer page/s, you're missing an opportunity to turn your visitors into leads.

What is the function of an offer page?

An offer page usually links to a sales campaign that targets a specific promotion, and the page's function is to take visitors and covert them into leads. By promoting a branded resource that pinpoints a specific problem your visitor struggles with, it's easier to convert visitors into leads. You can do this by promoting either a free or paid resource such as a downloadable whitepaper, event, eBook, report, video, webinar, form, checklist, or workbook in exchange for the visitor's contact information.

## How to measure its effectiveness

Sales offer pages include a clickable button that sends visitors to a shopping cart. Activity generated from offer pages can then be tracked to determine its effectiveness by analyzing click-through and conversion rates.

Now you know the definition of an offer page, its function, what it promotes, and how to track its success, you are ready to begin the courting process with your future customers.

When you were dating, did flowers, chocolates, or a special dinner at an elegant restaurant make an agreeable impression on your date? The same principal holds true in the marketing world. Design your gifts to move your visitor from the first date to a meaningful relationship.

## How to create a compelling offer page

### The power of one

If you give your prospects too many options and too many places to go, they'll become confused and overwhelmed and freeze. Your offer page should only make one offer and have one clickable button that takes them to one location.

### Never miss an opportunity for free marketing

Encourage your community to share links to your offer page. By allowing sharing, your visitors do the work of driving traffic to your website.

Is your content so good they can't resist?

Let's say you went out on a spectacular first date to a beautiful restaurant and your date was very impressed. Would you follow up on a second date by inviting your date to a car wash? I sure hope not! If you know your content offers tremendous value, great, you're on the right track. If not, make sure it does. Once you've set the bar, you need to continue wowing your prospects with your high-quality product/service at every stage of their buyer's journey.

## Be brief

Just like dating, if you ask too many questions and it begins to feel like a job interview, you'll scare your prospect off. Keeping your offer page to just one straightforward form with two-to-three fields increases your conversion rate.

## There's always room for improvement

Unless your offer page consistently generates more sales every month, there's always room for improvement. It's important to experiment with different landing pages to see which one/s give you the best results.

## Benefits of an offer page

Multiple offer pages with segregated offers will show you several important points; which topics are the most popular, which are the highest converting, and which channels your visitor's favor. These metrics are worth their weight in gold for helping you understand your audience and knowing which channels to focus your efforts.

As an example, if your date enjoyed dinner in a sophisticated restaurant but raved over the bouquet of peonies you gave her at dinner in a local diner, you know you should put your efforts into flowers and neighborhood eateries.

Lead magnets are also valuable for your visitors to gain a more thorough understanding of you, your product, and your business/service. Downloading quality content with your branding, is yet one more opportunity to create a good impression from multiple user experiences.

Your offer page is an excellent opportunity to turn visitors into leads, measure your products and campaigns' effectiveness, spread the word about your product/service, and create multiple quality branding experiences for your user.

Once you've made the effort to make an impressive impression on your first date, don't bypass the opportunity to turn that experience into a long-lasting relationship.

# CHAPTER 4
# AUTHENTICITY
# AND RELEVANCY

by Clate Mask, CEO & Co-founder of Keap

You might wonder why the CEO of a software company whose product does marketing automation would write a chapter about authenticity and relevancy in a digital marketing book?

And it's a fair question. Because after all, doesn't marketing automation—sending out the exact same email or text message to all of your contacts—stifle authenticity and risk being irrelevant?

Truthfully, if that's how a business is using marketing automation, "Yes." It absolutely does. And it happens because a time-impoverished entrepreneur may only see their options as binary:

- I can save time by sending an identical automated email to everyone on my list or...
- I can manually create custom emails for each contact.

This thinking, though common, reveals a lack of understanding of what it means to be "authentic" and "relevant".

First, according to Merriam-Webster, "authentic" means "true to one's own personality, spirit, or character" and "relevant" means" relating to a subject in an appropriate way".

But in the context of your business, what does that mean exactly?

At Keap, we work very hard at having our messaging about who we are, be authentic. On our website at Keap.com, our headline states:

> **"More sales. Fewer late nights. Grow without the chaos."**

and our subheadline is:

> **"From capturing and converting leads to making sure you get paid on time, Keap's all-in-one Sales & Marketing Automation (SMA) software helps you get more done in less time."**

The purpose is to clearly state who we are and what we can do to help small business owners. Those statements not only help potential customers understands what we can do for them, but they also guide our staff so that we can remain focused on those goals.

That authenticity reinforces in every employee at Keap our guiding principle; the importance of helping our customers grow their businesses, without remaining a slave to their business. Additionally, it ensures that all of our communications—whether by email, text message, or any other media—reflect those values.

Relevancy involves taking an authentic message and crafting it in a way that has the reader mentally say "Yes! That's me!".

Also, consider that because your messaging will be seen or heard by prospects that are potentially a bad fit for your product or service, authenticity and relevancy should also be used strategically to help prospects determine that your product or service may not be the right fit for them. This is an opportunity missed by many businesses and as a result, they squander resources on inferior prospects that either can not or should not buy from you.

So how does this apply to automation?

Think about your email inbox. Imagine you check your email and 3 emails have arrived since you last opened. You notice there is an email from your mom (or someone very close to you), there's another email from your Success Coach at Keap, and there's one from an unknown carpet cleaner that emails you every week about their "specials".

If you are like most people, you're going to open the personal email first and you will open it with almost no regard to the subject line. Why? Because you have intimate knowledge of the sender you can safely assume that the message from that person is going to be both authentic and relevant to you. The sender's personal status, authenticity and relevancy are assumed and you open their email with little or no hesitation.

In comparison, the email from your Keap Success Coach is not as likely to be opened solely on the strength of the sender's name. You may have had several interactions with your coach and deemed them to be authentically interested in the well-being of your business, but until you read the subject line, you will not determine if the email is potentially "relevant" and needs to be opened and read.

The last email is nothing but an advertisement for products or services offered by the carpet cleaner. No other useful information, just a sales pitch. And a week later, you get another email from them. And it's another sales pitch. And a week later, you get another email from them, and it's another sales pitch. These are the automated emails that are referred to as spam. They are neither authentic nor relevant yet this is the kind of communication that most businesses — wrongly — rely on.

Fortunately, there is a way to communicate with your prospects and customers that solves this problem and it begins with planning and watching their interactions with the content you're sending. Consider the following diagram:

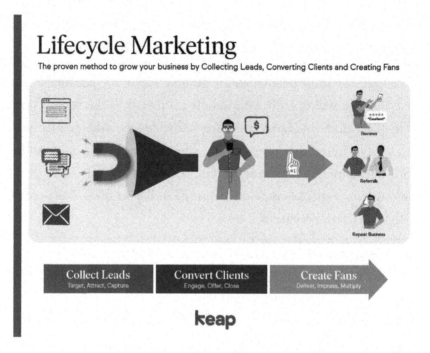

One of the first ways you can do this is with your lead capture. Again, let's use the carpet cleaner as an example. If you offered "The Dog Owner's Guide to Cleaning In-Home Pet Messes" you could assume that they likely have a dog or some other kind of pet if they requested it. Conversely, if you offered "3 Insider Secrets To Removing Toddler Art From Your Walls", it's likely they have young children.

When your prospect "clicks" to request the asset, you apply a tag to the contact record with something like "Profile — May have a dog" or "Profile — May have a toddler"

In the diagram, these are the three icons along the left side and represent different media like an email to a past prospect, a social media post, a mailed out postcard, etc. You'll be watching for the responses going to your landing page, requesting "the magnet" and you'll be recording that data.

**PRO TIP:** This is also why, in most cases, you should never drive paid traffic to a generic webpage. Your prospect is trying to solve a particular problem. If they have a dog that soiled the carpet and your Google Ad sends them to a generic home page that does not offer information about pet clean-up, they

are likely going to click the "back" button and leave. This is not just a loss for you because you paid for the click on Google, it's also a loss for your prospect because:

i. They didn't find information relevant to solving their problem and

ii. Because they left your website without leaving a name and email, you have lost the opportunity to show them how your business is unique and can solve cleaning problems in their home better than some other supplier.

## The Blue Funnel aka Engagement

You've had a request for your lead magnet and sent it to the prospect. Now it's time to start using the data you've been collecting to send out messaging that is authentic and relevant.

The first thing that would happen for the carpet cleaner would be to choose an engagement path for the prospect. The person that responded to the "dog mess clean-up" offer would be sent to a campaign where the automation talked about dogs and pets, the difficulties of cleaning up after them and the removal of stubborn odours. The person that responded to the "toddler clean-up" offer would not be sent down the pet campaign and would instead be sent information about toddler clean-ups, difficult cleaning challenges related specifically to children and how regular deep cleaning by the carpet cleaner would reduce dirt and bacteria in the house, thus keeping it cleaner and healthier for the toddler.

With each interaction, we could gather more information to further customize the material making it increasingly relevant to the prospects' needs. For example, if an email was sent with 2 videos — one related to smaller dogs and the other related to larger dogs, we would refine our messaging based on which video they chose to watch. Each interaction gives us additional information.

Now when an email goes out, it can read:

*Dear Donald, Accidents around the house happen and with larger dogs especially, those messes can be challenging. We understand. Since 1995, we're been cleaning up all kinds of pet-resident homes in Wichita and there's a good chance that you may even know some of them!...*

Compared to the generic *"Dear Homeowner, We clean carpets including pet stains, children's accidents, etc..."* the first email is not only to be far more relevant to the reader but you can authentically position your company as one that specialized in these kinds of solutions and promote your expertise.

All of this greatly improves your chances of being selected as the prospect's cleaner and getting the sale. (The middle of the diagram).

And that's it, right? On to the next prospect?

Smart business owners know that the first transaction is the beginning of the relationship, not the end.

Authenticity and relevancy should play a major role after the job is completed and you've been paid — an opportunity squandered by most business owners.

When your cleaning crew was at the client's home they had an opportunity to note other services that they could provide — furniture, drapes, hardwood floor refurbishment, throw rugs, and more.

You could easily customize ongoing follow-up — polling your new customer and ensuring they are happy with the service they received from your crew. By using data, you could list the items or areas that were serviced by your staff while omitting items that were not cleaned. Then you could use that data to either request a review on a third-party platform like Google or Facebook, request a referral, or suggest a service that you saw they could use, but had not yet purchased.

Additionally, because we know that people like to associate with other people like themselves, owners of dogs likely know other owners of dogs and parents of toddlers know other parents of toddlers. For that reason, you should be sending your customers a few additional "lead magnets". You would suggest that since they were happy with your products or services, friends, family, neighbours, and co-workers would be as well. Would they be willing to pass along the lead magnet to any of those people and state "these are the cleaners we use and they were great!"

Would that grow a business? Obviously, it would.

In the past, this has been extremely difficult for small businesses to do, but now with software like Keap, this kind of data collection is fairly easy to incorporate into your sales processes. As you collect information on your prospects and customers, you can easily move your prospects along different pathways that speak to their needs and wants plus you'll be able to show them what they can expect when they do business with your company.

The reality is that at Keap, we've worked hard to make the democratization of your data easy. Never has software made it easier for a small and medium-sized business to get deep psychographic insights into your customers' behaviours and predispositions.

Our partner, eLaunchers has created a special offer just for the readers of this book. When you visit https://www.elaunchers.com/justbuykeap you'll not only have the opportunity to acquire Keap at a special price and with additional users and contacts, you'll also receive:

- FREE 5 Funnels That Have Generated Over $5,000,000 In Revenue To Date & Counting — by eLaunchers.com

- FREE Marketing Automation Campaign — Business Kamasutra by eLaunchers.com (Over 500 installations worldwide)

- FREE Swipe Copy for Campaign, Funnels and Lead Magnets from eLaunchers.com

- FREE Migration from wherever you are to Keap by Keap Migration team.

**Go to https://www.elaunchers.com/justbuykeap and claim your free gifts today.**

Clate Mask is the Co-Founder and CEO of Keap CRM Software and lives with his wife Charisse in Chandler AZ.

# CHAPTER 5
# THE ASK FUNNEL

Imagine you find yourself at Bed, Bath, and Beyond. You are not shopping for anything in particular; you're just wandering around because you want to get out of the house and love Bed, Bath, and Beyond. Suddenly, a salesperson springs out of the bath aisle and starts peppering you with questions; What item are you looking for? Shower curtains, bath accessories, home decor, how about a throw and a couple of pillows? Are you aware of the benefits of our terry cloth bathrobes? Do you know they're on sale? Have you seen the sales rack?

Does it make you want to buy something or run out of the store as fast as your feet can carry you?

Unfortunately, the above scenario is the approach most web marketers take when they sell their products. They try to sell you something before knowing what you want.

But, you might ask, what if you don't know what you want? After all, you just wandered into Bed, Bath, and Beyond with no particular agenda.

Have you ever attended a tradeshow where the salesperson had a booth that advertised something so intriguing that you just had to know more?

*"Knives-so-sharp can slice your leather shoe in half just like butter."*

59

Would a booth that advertises the above knives pique your curiosity? You might not have come to the trade show to buy a super sharp knife, but you're pretty curious about whether that knife can actually cut a shoe in half. So, you stay for the demonstration.

While you're there, the salesperson asks you if you like cooking. That leads to a conversation about what type of cooking you most enjoy and which knives you use to prepare food. Then they ask you if you get frustrated with dull knives and the slow cutting process. They ask if you would like to learn how to cut some fancy vegetable patterns?

Suddenly, you realize you do not have one knife in your house that is sharp enough to cut shoes in half! You realize you simply cannot live without that super sharp Knives-so-sharp knife. While you're at it, because the salesperson is offering you a buy one get two for ½ price. maybe your sister and best friend could use one too. But they can only give you that price now, because they had so much fun talking to you....and it's the end of their day, and they don't want to pack all those knives back into their car.

While you're poised with debit card in hand, you notice a rack of low-priced colorful cutting boards and knife protectors. You decide to pick up a couple of cutting boards, why not, they're only a few bucks? You also spot a really nice knife set/knife rack combination at a higher price. The salesperson mentions that since you're already bought three knives, you qualify for a 59% discount. You decide to pick it up and give it as a gift to your parents for Christmas because this product is not available in stores.

That, my friends, is the right way to get to know your prospects and make an offer. It's called an "Ask Funnel," and it has a highly effective formula you can follow to help your future prospects see a solution to a problem they never knew existed.

### Step 1: Create a survey

Chances are there are three or four types of people who buy your products/services. Using the knife example, your segmented list may include:

- people who like to cook
- people who like to buy cooking accessory gifts for family or friends
- people who like to buy specialty kitchenware
- people who like novelty kitchenware

### Step 2: Create a simple survey question that engages all four types of customers in a conversation.

For example, "Who does the cooking in your household?" might provide multiple answers, such as my husband, my wife, my kids..

Once they've responded, potential prospects can be segmented into specific groups and taken to your landing page.

### Step 3: Your landing page must have a captivating headline.

It has got to be so interesting, that they want to find out more. From there, you can discuss the survey goal, and add a short video that builds your trust, credibility, and establishes you as the expert.

## Step 4: Ask more specific survey questions based on their segment.

- What type of knife materials do they prefer? Why?
- What type of edge retention are they in quest of?
- How tough do they want the knife to be?
- What type of ease of maintenance are they in search of?

## Step 5: Create a highly targeted sales pitch specific to that segment's niche.

For example, Knives-so-sharp is a must-have for the gourmet chef who demands a razor-sharp precision tool that provides both durability, and graceful control.

## Step 6: Agitate with a deep dive into their problem. In this example you're literally twisting the knife (pun intended).

For example, Are you frustrated with knives that become instantly dull, have rough and chipped cutting edges, that make you lose control so you hurt yourself while cooking, and what's worse, that create inconsistent, sloppy-looking food?

## Step 7: Describe your solution.

Knives-so-sharp is made of the highest quality carbon Cr17 stainless steel, corrosion-resistant blades that provide perfect precision control and balance. Knives-so-sharp features a meticulously hand-carved wooden handle with an index finger hole for superior control. The blade is forged with Japanese steel which ensures a sharp, long-lasting knife for years of enjoyment and comfort.

### Step 8: Create urgency for resolving the problem with your solution.

Buy Knives-so-sharp within the next hour and receive a 50% discount. Offer expires at 2:00 p.m. MST. The curved blade and finger hole elegantly fit into your hand, allowing you to never squash another tomato or give up on mincing herbs again. With Knives-so-sharp slicing through meat is a breeze, and cooking is easier and more fun.

### Step 9: While they are still in buying mode, upsell.

Your discount has been applied, and with your purchase you can also receive:

- 4 Knives-so-sharp paring knives for ~~$192.00~~      $47.00
- 3 Knives-so-sharp boning knives for ~~$165.00~~     $78.00
- 2 Knives-so-sharp bread knives for ~~$120.00~~      $60.00
- 1 Knives-so-sharp utility knife for ~~$72.00~~       $36.00

### Step 10: No sale? Rinse and repeat the "Ask-Funnel" formula from the beginning. Some potential prospects need a little more time, nurturing, and prompting to convert.

No one wants a generic email, or a long boring survey geared to the masses. The "Ask Funnel" provides a highly effective personalized experience for the future prospect, followed up by a customized offer.

# CHAPTER 6
# THE MEET FUNNEL/AKA THE DISCOVERY CALL

I receive a lot of emails from "website developers," "business development consultants," and many others who identify themselves as industry experts who attempt to sell me their web services.

The one I got this morning really annoyed me. It was from someone who identified herself as "Sophia," asking if I would be interested in redesigning my existing website. Her last sentence asked, "When could we schedule a call?" The thing is, why would I hire someone:

- I've never met

- I know nothing about

- Who hasn't identified "her" first or last name, business name, contact information, or business website?

- Who has no knowledge of my business goals, needs, or frustrations and has never bothered to find out?

- Who has not provided any evidence of experience, results, or a portfolio link?

- Who didn't bother to identify me by my first or

last name, or business name in the email?

• Who has poor grammar and spelling?

The final nail in the coffin — the website she was offering to redesign is offline because I closed that business in 2020.

Before you think this chapter will be one long gripe-fest, don't worry, it's not.

"Sophia" did an excellent job of demonstrating how to mess up each step in the "meet funnel" before requesting a discovery call. Unfortunately, Sophia is not alone. "A B2B SaaS company discovered their sales reps spent 70% of their day leaving voicemails that were never returned." (Source: Spotio, Sales Statistics, 2021).

What if you reversed the statistics and your sales reps got 70% of their business from discovery calls? Would that help your bottom line?

Trust for most people is not a given; you must earn it over time. Each of your actions within your meet funnel should create credibility, authenticity, and establish your expertise. The prospect's journey starts with your cold page, travels to your warm page, then to your hot page. Once prospects have arrived at your lead magnet page, you should have identified and described their pain points accurately enough that they are willing to give you their contact information in exchange for your resources.

But the secret sauce throughout this process is your genuine desire to solve their problem. Only then will they agree to a discovery call and trust your intention to provide them with a valuable service. As you know, the journey to gaining a thorough understanding of your prospect's problem and gaining their trust follows a series of steps.

## 1. Do your homework!

How impressed would you be with an applicant who showed up for an interview and knew absolutely nothing about your company? You might even send them on their way without completing the interview. Take the time to research your prospect's business so that you can fine-tune your message and products to their needs.

## 2. Become an outstanding listener

Your discovery call is an opportunity to learn about their goals and to see if your product/service aligns with their objectives. Asking short specific questions will uncover valuable information about your prospect's business. Take care to listen carefully to their responses. If your product doesn't fit their business, you've done your best and can disqualify them. I'm a firm believer in exercising good karma, and I will happily refer prospects to a service that meets their goals, even if it's not mine. If during your call you discover your product is a fit, you're ready to move to the next step.

To get you started with your informational mining expedition, try these five questions:

    i.   Whenever your prospect makes a general or vague statement, ask "why"? You may be surprised what that one small word can uncover.

    ii.  Ask for clarification. If a prospect says, we've had a horrible month; ask, "can you clarify why this month has been so horrible for your business?"

    iii.  The second layer of asking a clarifying question is to uncover the personal impact of the problem with a simple question. "How did your bad month affect you personally?" From their response, you will uncover issues they are dealing with and assess their weight as a prospect.

iv.  The third layer of questioning is to ask them to tell
      you more. This open-ended question encourages
      your prospect to provide more details and context.

v.   Have you ever noticed how uncomfortable people
      are with silence? People talk to fill the void. Remind
      yourself to treat their silence like gold and allow them
      the space to speak. There's a good chance they will
      tell you something you hadn't thought of asking.

## 3. Clarify, clarify, clarify

Use the discovery call as a chance to clarify and summarize
your prospect's pain points. Once you've demonstrated your
understanding, you can explain how your product/service is a logical
solution to their problems.

## 4. Create strategic goals

Nothing is a bigger turnoff than buying a product/service, only to
have the salesperson disappear after the sale. Think carefully about
how you can continue working with your prospect to help them
achieve their goals over their business's lifespan. By doing this, you
acknowledge their value as your customer while supporting them
in achieving long-term success. A long-term strategic goal builds
your credibility and establishes an ongoing root structure for your
relationship to grow.

## 5. Provide immediate next steps

At the end of your discovery call, your prospect should have a
checklist with dates for their next steps. Take a proactive approach
and schedule their actions into your calendar to facilitate the process
and nurture the relationship along its path.

Following these five steps in the Meet Funnel ensures you and your prospect look forward to your discovery call. It also establishes you as a person/business who genuinely cares about your customers and is willing to make the effort for their long-term success.

# CHAPTER 7

# THE REFERRAL PAGE

A few years ago, I asked my barber what he did to market his business. He answered in one word. Referrals.

When I started a new sub-business about five years ago, I got all my new clients through referrals from my business networking group. My wife's nail salon offers 20% off the sixth visit. Evernote awards points for referrals. Uber's rideshare program rewards both the referrer and the referee with a free ride for each newly activated account. Even Google offers a $15 cash incentive for each new Google Apps for Work account activated.

Referrals are one of the most crucial and reliable methods of growing a business. If you're new to the concept of a referral funnel, it's easy to grasp. Generating a successful referral funnel involves a two-step process:

i.   Identify your best referral partners and educate them about your ideal customer.

ii.  Follow systematically implemented referral strategies.

## Who is your ideal referral partner?

Every business has no less than five referral categories. These are people within your personal and business range with whom you share a co operative relationship. For example, suppose you are a realtor. Your referral categories would include mortgage brokers, real estate lawyers, former satisfied clients, property managers, family, friends, church/community, networking groups, and services such as tradespeople, dry cleaners, etc. These are the people you are already giving your time, talents, and business to. The people in your referral circle know, like, and trust you. You also know like and trust them. When someone asks a person in your relationship circle for an introduction to a good realtor, they refer you.

### Make sure it's a two-sided relationship

As with any relationship, if it's one-sided with one person doing all the giving and the other person doing all the taking, it is bound to fail. I'm happy to refer people to my barber because he's given me great cuts for years. If he weren't my barber, I wouldn't feel comfortable referring to him or his business. The same holds true for your referral partners; the more value you provide to their business, the more likely they are to refer business to you.

### Are you a match?

Would I keep going back to my barber if he gave great cuts, but I couldn't stand his personality? Not likely. Not everyone is your type and they don't have to be. There is enough work in the world for all of us.

### Do they know what you do and how you do it?

Set up a coffee date or zoom meeting with your referral partner to explain what you do and how you help your clients. In turn, your referral partner can tell you the same about their business. A meeting fills in the information gaps. It also establishes trust, credibility and ensures you both feel more comfortable sending people each other's way.

## Have you painted a crystal-clear picture of your ideal referral?

Many times, we assume people who know us can automatically identify our ideal referral. If we haven't told them, how will they know? This is where the adage "specific is terrific" fits in. An example for a realtor: An ideal referral for me is a young professional couple who have been renting and are now getting married. They want to buy a house so they can start a family. By painting a picture of your ideal referral, you have alerted their radar to your ideal referral customer.

## Now it's your turn to reciprocate

The reason Evernote, Uber, and Google's referral programs work so well is because they reciprocate. Their "thank you" system rewards their customers for referrals. You might not want to send money or give away gifts yet. However, the best way to thank your referral partner is to send business their way when you're starting. Ask them who their ideal referral customer is and keep your antenna out.

Once you've established your ideal customer, you and your referral partner can specify how you would like to be connected. Is an email introduction your favorite introduction? Or would you rather have a phone call or meet in person?

## Referral Strategies

Now that you've identified and educated your referral partner, it's time to implement your referral strategies.

    iii. Reframe. If asking for referrals makes you cringe or is confusing, reframe it to something more palatable, like an introduction. Next time you meet up with your referral partner, ask for an introduction to your ideal client (rather than a referral) and see what happens.

iv.  Practice makes permanent. Asking for help is something many people struggle with; however, with practice, it becomes easy and natural. You'll discover people like to help, especially if it's a friend or colleague.

v.   Include everyone in your network. Make a list of everyone in your sphere, include hobbies, children's teachers or coaches, alumni, neighbors, clients—everyone. It's a numbers game; the more people you know and ask, the more referrals you'll get.

vi.  Set SMART goals. Defining your goals is great, especially if they're specific, measurable, achievable, realistic, and timely. Writing them down is even better. But holding yourself accountable wins the trophy. Whether that means scheduling them in your online calendar or CRM, or calling your accountability partner once a week, setting goals and holding yourself accountable will achieve results.

vii. Host customer-only (and guests) events. Who doesn't love being treated like a V.I.P? Exclusive events are ideal for your network to invite people within their network. Events sharpen your network's radar to people would benefit from your event and your product/service. Exclusive customer-only events give your clients and prospects the message that they are valuable. You'll also find existing customers do your selling for you. How great is that?!

Unless you're already drowning in business and can't possibly take on another new client, having an effective referral funnel should be a central part of your business strategy.

# PART 3

# Squeeze
# Pages

# CHAPTER 8

# HOW ABOUT A LITTLE SQUEEZE? (PAGE)

With all the mobile messengers, apps, and chat boxes, isn't email fading away? According to Statistica, a data analysis company, in 2020, there were approximately 306 billion emails sent worldwide every day. That number is projected to increase to over 376 billion by 2025.

It looks like email is here to stay.

Let's consider another statistic. For every $1 spent, email generates $38 (Source Hubspot: The Ultimate List of Email Marketing Stats for 2020, Forsey, Caroline, 2020). For a 3,800% return on your investment, would it be worth your while to create a tool that captures emails for your potential prospects?

Your business needs a tool that captures leads that convert into email subscribers and eventually paying customers. A squeeze page does the trick.

It's called a squeeze page because its sole purpose is to squeeze contact information from your website visitors, so that you can generate leads.

Squeeze pages and landing pages often get confused. The main difference is that a squeeze page has only one goal and one page, whereas a landing page can have multiple goals on one page. For example, a squeeze page's only goal is to capture the visitor's email address. In contrast, a landing page can ask a visitor to sign up for a webinar, download a resource such as a whitepaper or a report, or sign up for a free trial of a product/service.

A squeeze page can fit neatly into any area of your website; your home page, blog page, any place that grabs your visitor's attention. It persuades prospects to part with their contact information in exchange for a valuable resource.

A squeeze page has very few elements which include:

- A headline
- Supporting text with a Call to Action Button (CTA) and testimonials
- A form with a couple of fields that capture the visitor's name and email address
- A thank you page
- Content offers (eBooks, whitepapers, webinars, courses, reports, etc.)

All well-oiled machines have automated processes, and your squeeze page should too.

Are you paying attention? Doing this makes you money!

Did that heading get your attention? It should, your squeeze page headline should grab your visitor's attention and identify a benefit.

AND — never miss an opportunity to squeeze your branding onto the page.

What's next?

Following the heading is your supporting text, which should flush out all the information your visitor needs to decide. It's best to keep it to one page and to the point. Include the CTA button in a prominent place and color with plenty of white space around the image. A good use of the CTA is to highlight what they'll get. "Get your free tips." Yes! Download my forms." "Send my report."

People love proof and adding a few testimonials from happy customers helps convince your new customers to share their contact information.

Then what?

The form can make or break your squeeze page. If you ask for too much information before your visitor has had a chance to get to know you/ your product, you'll frighten them away. Make sure to only ask for the information you need to justify receiving the content. Typically, a name and an email address are enough. Although if you require more information and can justify it, your form can have additional fields, or you can send your visitors to a second squeeze page.

I like to use the dating analogy. If you are out on a first date and ask too many questions, your date may begin to feel like they are being interrogated and want to run away. The courtship needs to be a pleasant process of gradual engagement.

## Say thanks

The thank-you page should pop up right after your customer has filled out and submitted their form. Since saying thank you is the last step in the conversion process and it's essential to include. The anatomy of a thank you page provides confirmation they completed the form, the value they'll receive from your product, and assurance there is a person on the other end of the message.

Give them their product—fast!

According to chilipiper.com, an automation software tech business, the cogs in the wheel need to start turning within five minutes of receiving the contact information. If you don't get back to your potential customer in 5 minutes or less, your competitor will. Five minutes is the sweet spot.

About a year ago, I was looking for a handyman to fix a crack in my basement foundation. Initially, I did a google search and called a handful of companies. None of them got back to me. Next, I ventured onto a landlord Facebook group for my area and asked for referrals. Within minutes I had eight recommendations. I called all eight, "Moe" got back to me within minutes. We had a great conversation, and I hired him immediately. Since then, he's my trusted "go-to" guy for everything maintenance—related. By the way, one other handyman got back to me two weeks later (long after I hired Moe).

Moe's response time won him about $10K in business just from me this year. I plan to keep hiring him until I sell the house.

## A little extra

The thank-you page can also:

- display your navigation menu to keep customers connected to your website

- link to additional relevant content (to warm customers to future buying)

- provide an opportunity to share with social media (do remember to display your social media icons prominently)

- have a possible second CTA to a form that mirrors the length of the offer's value (a short form = a quick one-item offer). Don't make the mistake of offering too much to start. Let visitors ease into a relationship, by only giving them what the need and can consume in a few minutes.

A Squeeze page is an essential tool in your Pixel Estate. Squeeze pages can convert leads into customers by educating, guiding, and building trust. They extend your social reach and provide valuable content as your new lead progresses through the buyer's journey.

# CHAPTER 9

# THE CALL
# TO ACTION

**Read to the end of this chapter to receive $1 million!**

Now that you're motivated to read to the end, I'll share my insights on how to encourage your users to engage.

You created an insightful and informative newsletter, blog posts bursting with priceless content, and the most user-friendly shopping cart imaginable. So, why aren't your prospects buying your products?

As many of you know, I was on faculty at the University of Phoenix. My experience teaching students taught me that my students couldn't read my mind, I had to tell them exactly what to do. I also had to tell them what to expect when they followed instructions, with a clear, direct message. In the military this message is called a direct command, in marketing it's called a Call to Action or CTA.

A call-to-action (CTA) on your website is a button with a phrase that triggers your prospective customers to take action to download a resource in exchange for their contact information. An irresistible CTA phrase is specific, urgent, and makes the user act.

Once your prospect clicks the CTA and have been added to your email list, they start to move through your buyer's journey. CTAs should be obvious, striking, action-oriented, and easy to find on your web pages and emails.

There are 10 key points to remember when creating your CTA.

i. **Get to the point as quickly as possible and in 35 characters or less.** This is your chance to tell your audience precisely what to do. The easier it is to understand what to do and what they'll receive, the higher your click rate.

"Buy here" or "shop now" are great CTA's for an e-commerce site. "Subscribe" or "download now" are effective CTAs for a newsletter or a content sample. "Start my free 30-day trial" could be used for a product trial.

ii. **If you want an enthusiastic response, write an enthusiastic CTA.**

Let's look at two examples:

• "Click here for information on booking your next family vacation."

Does this CTA create excitement?

• "Click here to plan your family dream vacation today!"

This second CTA sounds more appealing and creates urgency and the exclamation mark adds excitement. Just make sure not to overuse the exclamation marks, or they'll blend into the woodwork and have the opposite effect of what you want.

iii. **Create urgency.**

We are bombarded with massive content every day, and this makes it easy to let anything that isn't urgent slip in-between the cracks.

Example, "Only 5 free consultants left — call today." This CTA demonstrates scarcity (only 5 free consultations left) and creates urgency (call today).

iv. **Implement a self-service appointment scheduler.**

The fewer the steps, the easier the process, and the higher the conversion. When you've decided on a product/service, do you really want to click through three pages to schedule a phone call? You don't want a process that makes your customers lose patience. Customers have a much better experience by instantly scheduling their own appointments. A study by Forrester found 72% of customers prefer self-service over phone/email support.

v. **Create a document library.**

Suppose a customer is researching both your website and two competitor's websites. You all have convincing website content, catchy CTA's, and solid industry credentials. The one difference is your website has a free content library that provides the most up-to-date and relevant information in downloadable videos, PDFs, eBooks, and tutorials. Who wins? According to Seismic, 90% of customers are more likely to buy from the company that provides the most relevant information.

A document library is also good for your company's team members who can access pooled resources and share them across multiple channels.

vi. **Create fear of missing out FOMO.**

I get these "only today, act now" messages
all the time, and I still fall for them. If I'm
shopping for a product I want, I absolutely
do not want to miss out on the sale price!

Your content can describe the pain points and
the consequences of not taking advantage of your
product or service; then, your CTA can mention a
time-sensitive sale or promotion. "Sale ends today
at 5:00 p.m. MST." "Only 30 left, buy now!"
Amazon is good at creating urgency by displaying
limited numbers of items with messages like;
"only 2 left in stock." It always works on me.

vii. **Understand your customer's device behaviour.**
Did you know how people search and what they
search for are specific to the device? According to
a study conducted in 2021 by Broadbandsearch.
net, "the e-commerce conversion rate for desktops
was 4.81% while the rate for mobile devices was
only 2.25%." They also noted that big online
purchases are made on a desktop and smaller/
impulse purchases are made on a mobile device.
Most social media is done on mobile devices.

That said, do you have clear CTAs configured
for impulse mobile device purchases and specific
CTAs created for the larger ticket items bought
from desktop devices? Make sure you do.

viii. **Keep your CTAs fresh and creative.**
Although you might love your tried and true

CTA, it's essential to try out a couple of examples of CTAs to see which perform the best.

Instead of; "try out todays' deals," add a little spice with; "smokin' deals with a click of your fingertips." Or, instead of "complete your information to get started," give it a shot of caffeine with; "Yes! I want great health today!"

ix. **Show the numbers.**

When searching for a product or service, I know my budget and start my search by comparing similar products with pricing information. If it's a crazy price, I'll move on. If it's within my budget, I'll stay on the site. Customers behave in the same way. Once they've seen your pricing and remain on your website, you know they're still interested, and you stand a good chance of gaining a conversion.

"Shop today for CRM's under $500" shows the price range and creates urgency. "Book your next appointment today to receive 20% off your next haircut." My hairdresser has an ongoing promo; when I book my next 2 appointments, my name is entered in a draw for a free haircut. I've never won yet, but I keep trying.

x. **Do the opposite.**

You might feel a little queasy doing this, but talking trash gets attention.

For clients with gum disease who dread going to the dentist, "Does your spouse say you have bad breath? I can help," pushes the pain buttons

and prompts action. For lawn care, "do you have
the ugliest yard on your street? We can fix it,"
might make customers pick up the phone.

You may have already guessed I'm not going to give you $1 million
for reading this chapter. Sorry. But by implementing, practicing,
and observing the 10 key points, your CTAs will grab your visitor's
attention and nudge them through your buyer's journey so you can
make your own $1 million.

# CHAPTER 10
# THE PILLAR PAGE

A pillar page is one web page that covers all aspects of a general topic in depth and that links to clusters or pillars of related content.

## Think like a search engine

To understand the importance of a pillar page, it's essential first to recognize how people search for information.

Back in the day when search engines were new, you would type one word in the search bar. Say you were looking for a dentist, you'd type "dentist." From there, you'd narrow down your search results to "local," "periodontists," etc., to find a specialized dentist in your area.

Today, you'd type your first search query as "periodontists near me, highest ratings." Why? Because according to Ahrefs: Long Tail Keywords, which are queries of four words or more, help 64% of the web population find the precise information they're seeking.

People would rather quickly skim through specific topics to find exact information rather than waste their time sorting through tons of content. Now, when you type in "dentists" in the search bar, Google shows you results for dentists, periodontists, and top-rated local dentists. Search engines these days know their consumers and are configured to deliver the most highly rated and accurate results on linked topics.

Now back to your pillar page. Because of the way search engines operate, your website needs to organize content by main cluster topics. Then, those topic cluster blogs hyperlink to long-tail keywords. Following this method allows search engines to address as many queries as possible specific to your subject areas.

## Create your pillar page

To create your pillar page content, go back to your clients/audience. You know them because you work with them every day. What are their challenges? What are their interests? Choose a topic that identifies their top issue and is broad enough to break into in-depth cluster blogs.

Suppose you are a periodontist. Your pillar page could consist of a long-form blog post on dental health and how it relates to overall physical and mental health. Within your blog, hyperlink your cluster topics. When readers click the hyperlinks, the cluster blogs offer a deep dive into each specific topic area covered in your pillar content. Sample cluster topics might include gingivitis, gum decay, bone loss, heart disease, changes to facial appearance, and self-esteem, to name a few. When your audience is reading through your pillar page, if they find specific topics they'd like to learn more about, they click the hyperlinks.

## Create Topic Clusters

Search engines love topic cluster models. Topic clusters unify your content and eliminate multiple blog posts on the same topic and competing URLs within your website. To create a topic cluster;

1. Choose a wide-ranging topic where you'd like to rank

2. Create blog articles based on specific, linked, topic keywords

3. Organize your clusters into three components:

    a. Pillar content

    b. Cluster content

    c. Hyperlinks

Gone are the days of "any content is good content" and keyword stuffing. Google's algorithms constantly change and evolve, as have the way people search for information. Knowing how search engine algorithms operate gives you key insight into writing and organizing your pillar content and cluster areas. This, in turn, improves your search engine ratings and user experience.

# CHAPTER 11

# PUTTING IT ALL TOGETHER

I f you've read this far and your head isn't swimming—congratulations!

But, if you've read this far and your head IS swimming—I'm still going to congratulate you because this is really a lot of information to take in!

Building an effective, efficient, and dynamic website involves many components, including: creating the right types of pages, writing great search engine optimized content that attracts prospects, producing products that fill a need, maintaining and segregating your email lists of prospects and clients for targeted marketing, positioning your content strategically, and lastly implementing automated processes.

## How To Build Your Website And CRM

To accomplish these tasks, you have two choices:

    i.   Create a website and corresponding spreadsheets, various software applications, rely on staff members to store customer information in their memory and on separate databases, and hope all the bits and pieces accommodate a makeshift customer relationship management (CRM) program. Then, when your business expands, search for plugins to integrate the various systems or search for a new CRM system.

ii.   Integrate your website with a CRM system from day 1.

This type of system assimilates all the functionalities of your website, handles inbound/outbound marketing, sales, coverts lead and closes customers, and can grow and expand with your business when needed.

Obviously, the first alternative is piecemeal, which opens your business up for missed opportunities, knowledge gaps, and staff withholding or losing information and business. Additionally, it creates disruption and chaos — even lost business when moving from multiple systems, people, and platforms to one platform.

It's not a criticism, it's the reality of being an entrepreneur. When you're starting your business, you're so busy figure out what balls to keep in the air and then keeping them in the air that you grab quick solutions as problems arise.

Over time, more issues pop up, and so do software fixes. Because they are not designed to be integrated, you cobble them together with various third-party applications.

Patching up all the little things that continually break down becomes more expensive in the long run than if you had paid for one or two more significant programs with a couple of vendors. It also becomes a nightmare to support because vendors don't necessarily know how to or want to support each others' programs.

Eventually, your system will break down and harm or destroy your business efficiency and growth. Sooner or later, you will have to face the music and rebuild your website and CRM starting with a blueprint of your business plan, marketing strategy, buyers' journey, and user workflow.

The second alternative puts your business in the right position to expand and grow while integrating the various inbound and outbound sales/marketing systems used to attract visitors, covert leads, and close customers. From the onset, you and your staff work with effective marketing that collects information about your prospects from multiple channels such as web page activity, social media, and the type of content that interests them while engaging various channels to build an ongoing relationship. Implementing an integrated system from the start helps you grow your business, build customer loyalty, and keeps you and your business organized.

## An Integrated System

An integrated system supports you in:

- Knowing how to create a constant crop of leads
- Understanding who should be nurturing your prospects at which phase of their growth
- Recognizing your client's needs from their digital fingerprint across multiple channels
- Scaling up successful lead tactics

An integrated inbound marketing software enables:

- Easy publishing for search engine optimized, appropriate, appealing blog content
- Optimized, personalized landing pages
- Tailored emails, content, and subject lines

Lead management

- Sales-ready focused campaigns
- Analytics for social media, SEO, calls-to-action, and advertisements that let you measure and assess your customer progress and your ROI
- Synchronization of datasets for easy access to emails, CTA's, forms, and segmented lists

When marketing operates in a silo, productivity suffers. For marketing to produce a healthy crop of flourishing customers, it requires a unique, integrated, organic system specific to the customer within a multi-channel dynamic ecosystem.

## I Love it But I Can't Afford It

At this point, you might be saying, "I love the concept of an integrated system, but I'm just getting started and I don't have tons of money to invest."

You'll be happy to know, we have an excellent integrated website/ CRM system and can work with just about any kind of budget since we offer three tiers of support. We offer these three tiers because we want you to get your business off on the right foot, and we want to support you from the beginning and through every step of your business growth.

Yes You Can!

The three tiers include the:

     i.   Starter

    ii.   Professional

   iii.   Enterprise

For the complete novice who does not yet have a website, the Starter provides exceptional value by offering a fast, secure, reliable website, complete content management, and an all-in-one CRM platform.

For a business that wants a system to attract and engage traffic, the Professional offers all the same features as the Starter with the bonus personalized customer experience, optimization, content strategy, and extended functionality with Salesforce integration, 25 Dashboards, and access to Hubspot's replatforming services.

For a large, established business that wants to create powerful user experiences such as memberships and web apps, manage their growing team and brand, and add multi-domain traffic reports and additional brand domains, the Enterprise checks all the boxes.

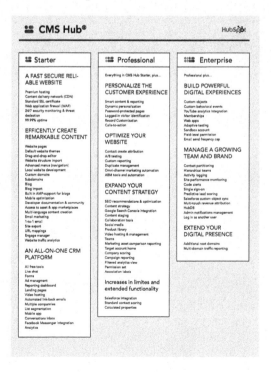

Our team will set up the command & control center and the communications processes to implement your efficient website and CRM system. Our process gets things done fast and right the first time, staying on time and budget. Most importantly, the implementation plan brings an order, discipline, and customer-focused workflow to your inbound and outbound marketing, sales, and customer service.

My end goal is to have your website turn attraction into prospects that become leads, which convert into lifelong customers. If that sounds like something you'd like for your business, I'd like to help. When you're successful, I'm successful.

If I can be of service to you, I'd like to know-how.

Best wishes as you follow your journey to success.

# FREQUENTLY ASKED QUESTIONS

I am frequently asked the same questions from business owners interested in automating their GDD Pixel Estates, so I wanted to include some of those questions to help you understand how we can work together.

**Q** **What is eLaunchers?**

A. eLaunchers is a turnkey marketing communication firm that offers data-centric automated marketing that integrates email, social media, online marketing, offline marketing, and telephone marketing. Our system creates lead generation, lead capture, and lead conversion from one central location.

It drives prospects to a squeeze page on the homepage, a campaign-specific-URL, or a personalized URL.

It coaxes a prospect to leave their name, email, and phone number, captures and stores their information, and builds a sales funnel that nurtures leads into lifelong customers. The sales funnel can lead up to an initial appointment or a long-term, nuture program.

**Q** **Who is your ideal client?**

A. My ideal clients are professionals who realize the importance of having an efficient, automated sales funnel that creates lead generation, lead capture, and lead conversion. Typically, I work well with companies that are spending money on marketing but are unhappy with the results.

The process we build inserts devices in your current marketing materials that helps you determine what is and isn't working. That way, you can go in and figure out what to do to turn on the heat or what to tone down or turn off.

Q How do I know your system works?

A. I've been in direct marketing since 1989 and have helped small to not-so-small businesses and organizations compete and win against rivals with colossal marketing dollars.

Since 2002 I've been helping entrepreneurs and business owners build and automate their marketing campaigns by leveraging technology. I have a long and fruitful track record (19 years and counting) of supporting business owners in my community. My clients range from well-known, high-profile direct marketers to local dentists and chiropractors, among many other professionals. We have mailed over a billion pieces of direct mail, produced over 10,000 marketing campaigns, built over 1000 websites and landing pages, and generated over 1,000,000 Personalised URLs (PURLS).

During my MBA, I learned how to utilize the SWOT analysis method, analyzing your business' strengths, weaknesses, opportunities, and treats. It is a handy tool to address what works, what doesn't work, what is missing, how to minimize risks, and how to take the best advantage of success opportunities.

My process builds trust with prospects that develops into life-long client relationships that can be monitored, measured, and monetized. For real life case studies, check out my eLaunchers Testimonials and Case Studies https://www.magcloud.com/browse/issue/55600.

# Q How much does it cost?

A. It's expensive because it is a significant relationship that involves substantial time and attention from both of us. As mentioned in Chapter 14, it involves a three-step process.

## Phase I, Planning

This process usually takes anywhere from 1-12 days. Within that time, we define your business concepts and marketing strategy and complete your 73-point business-building checklist. From this information, we compile your 2-page marketing plan and plan your 3-5-year marketing roadmap, with annual priorities and quarterly Specific, Measurable, Attainable, Relevant, and Time-Bound (SMART) goals.

## Phase II, Design & Build

Magic happens here. We design your systems and processes for your website, blog, funnels, landing pages, and call to action through our marketing automation platform.

## Phase III, Deliver and Execute

In this phase, we deliver your online and offline marketing campaigns, document the findings, and assess which conversion methods work best for your business. We've discovered clients are all different. Some want inspirational articles with lots of images, others like to see comparisons from charts and graphs, and a third might only respond if you tug on their heartstrings. Documentation and trending help analyze what's working best for your business.

We outfits your business with the right processes and systems to take your prospects on a three-phase journey. The end goal is to turn attraction into prospects that become leads, which convert into lifelong customers.

At the time or writing, your total yearly investment is $87,000, paid in one of two ways:

    i.   The initial consult fee is $12,000 — which is a year-long process, and the implementation is sold separately for $8,750. The remainder of the payment you can pay with a set, small monthly paycheck.

    ii.  The initial consult fee is $12,000 — which is a year-long process, and the implementation is sold separately for $8,750. You decide how much to contribute to the monthly paycheck every month. How fast and how much work is accomplished depends on what you choose to pay monthly.

With both payment methods, all work to implement your fully automated system, which will be completed by the end of the year. The only difference is that with the 2nd payment method, you are in control of the amount you would like to pay monthly and the speed and amount of work you would like to have accomplished each month. We do whatever it takes to make you win.

All my services come with a 100%money-back guarantee. We do not guarantee success, and to be honest, I don't always achieve success. I don't have a silver bullet. What I do ensure is that if you are unhappy, that you request a refund. If that happens, I am perfectly willing to write off my losses and move on rather than lose a friend.

Q  Why do you have a monthly maintenance fee?

A. If you have the skills to manage an in-house or outsourced complex marketing machine with many moving parts, you won't need our monthly maintenance fee. If not, or you would instead focus on building your business, you will require us to do that work for you.

I have teams that allow me to deploy your marketing system 24/7. If you're driving home from work and you decide to call me to say, "I want to do change campaign number 23 to list segment 6 in the next two weeks." I can do that. That's why you pay a monthly maintenance fee.

## Q How long does it take?

A. The entire process can take anywhere between six weeks and six months, depending mainly on you.

## Q Who is in charge of the process?

A. We are. We have a dedicated project manager who runs the project and is in charge of the project management dashboard.

You, your staff, and the other vendors report to the master dashboard and the master task list.

## Q What do I have to do?

A. In a word. Lots. Putting an integrated automated sales and marketing system in place is a process that involves everyone's best efforts, you, your staff, and of course, us. But not to worry! We have procedures, systems, and applications in place that help you manage your workload. We're always there with you. We tell you exactly what needs to be done and put an expert beside you to complete the tasks.

You will either need to write or work with a writer that you hire. You will need to approve of the content and the strategy. You will also need to share your spirit that we then capture and share with the world. You will need to read what we give you and provide us with timely feedback.

We need to work as one cohesive force because you will need to put me in charge of your staff, who report to my project manager, my production manager, and my timeline when you buy my system.

Q Once this system is implemented, what work does my staff have to do?

A. We will discuss this in great detail during our first meeting. It depends on many factors, your staff, their technical aptitude, and what work the system assigns to people.

Most businesses follow this process:

- start with people
- give the person/people an apparatus
- assemble a workflow system
- as the business grows—add more people
- people bring their appliances and apparatuses
- data flows as an outgrowth of people, devices, and apparatuses

With my system, we start at the end, which puts people in control of the data. Here's how our process works:

- build a data system
- defer the apparatus to the data system
- defer people to the apparatus

Out of 465 things your marketing machine will do, 11-15 are assigned to people who have to do the work, such as learning and adopting the system, picking up the phone to call the prospect, and closing the deal. Your people are your single most significant asset.

## Q Why should I go through this?

A. The core purpose of implementing an automated marketing system is to reduce dependency on people. If you do not have an automated system you are always exchanging physical work for hourly dollars. You are also relying on people to get things done. Depending on the reliability, health, and attitude of the people who do the work, it may or may not get done, and the consistency will vary.

You want to do this because you can only do so much on your own without burning out. With an automated sales system, the marketing machine can work 24/7 to generate leads that can be channeled into your sales funnel that converts into sales.

## Q Do you do the printing?

A. Yes, we have a resident print production manager who will manage your printing, mailing, data processing, mail merge, and everything else. We do not own our print production facility. We work with a ½ dozen vendors we have built trusted relationships with over the years. We buy their services wholesale. For your production costs, you are paying for your project manager, the production manager's time, a small contribution to my overhead, and a small profit. The price is about 20-30% more than the market.

Our rule of thumb is that if a project is more extensive than $5000, it may make sense to ask one or more team members to coordinate and manage. If something goes wrong, we can take over the project and put it back on track.

Q **How do you generate leads?**

A. We generate leads through multiple methods:

- targeted email marketing
- external referral marketing (referral systems)
- online marketing
- social media
- targeted multi-step direct mail
- targeted every door direct mail
- internal client referral marketing
- external marketing
- free standing inserts
- pre-and post-event marketing

Q **What methods do you not use for sales and marketing?**

A. The methods we do not use are:

- radio
- television
- public relations
- space/print advertising
- outdoor advertising
- vehicle wraps

Q **Who develops the content?**

A. To answer this question, you'll have to bear with me while I rant for a little while.

Effective sales content should capture your style and tone while increasing your brand awareness and powers of persuasion. There is an art and a science to making it sound like it comes from your heart. It should not be taken lightly, nor should it be outsourced to a staff member with some writing skills to save time or money.

If you insist on writing your content, learn from the masters; Dan Kennedy or Robert Cialdini. As I have. Dan Kennedy's books show you the formulas he's used to make millions of dollars from copywriting. Learning his techniques takes practice; developing consistent skills takes years.

If you don't have the time or feel confident yet in your copywriting ability, we can outsource it to a skilled copywriter. Or if you'd instead choose your own, we are happy to provide referrals.

## Q What if I need videos?

A. Our consultation for determining what type of media you need is included in the fee. However, the video itself is an additional cost.

There are three types of videos:

    i. PowerPoint slides with voice added to them

    ii. Animated videos like the ones you see on my website

    iii. Professional shot and edited videos

Regardless of which one you choose; you will need to follow the same six processes:

    i. Define the purpose of your video

    ii. Create a video storyboard

     iii.  Choreograph the video

     iv.  Generate a draft of your video

     v.  Produce video scripts

     vi.  Rehearse

Either we can outsource the videographer, or if you have someone you like to work with, by all means, hire them. If you need to fly out to a studio, we can arrange that for you too.

**Q** **What are the most common mistakes people make when doing marketing on their own or hiring another firm?**

A. Glad you asked! There are three areas I've identified in my 19 years in the business:

     i.  Failing to plan. Creating a marketing plan is like writing an essay; you start with the end in mind or a goal and work backward. Planning extends to resources too, and you need to factor in the time, money, and resources required to deliver your project. You also need to set benchmarks or win conditions and, of course, the end goal.

     ii.  Lack of clear expectations of needs, objectives, the results, and the reasons why these things are essential.

     iii.  A lack of understanding of what constitutes successful implementation of a project and what constitutes failure of a project

**Q** **There are lots of marketing companies, why should I choose you?**

A. I don't claim to be the best at everything, but I do claim to be the best at understanding the correlation between data and money better than anybody else.

My goal is to make you two or three times as much money as you spent on my marketing consultation. Of course, like with everything else, I have a process for this.

But unlike everyone else, if you're not happy with the results, you can either have a do-over to see if we can do it better or have a 100% unconditional money-back guarantee.

Think about that.

Q What do you have to lose?

A. You've seen how I've worked with other businesses over 19 years to become a recognized expert.

You've heard how others have used our systems to reap the benefits of an integrated, automized system.

Now it's time for a decision.

The way I see it, you have three options:

    i.   Do nothing and stay precisely where you are now.
If you aren't convinced that having an GDD Pixel
Estate with an integrated, automated marketing
and sales system is critical in today's business
environment, you don't need our system.

But if you get that our system saves you time and money by automating your sales processes quickly and efficiently, you have two other options;

ii.  Do it yourself. Hire all the people and find all the processes to implement your automated sales and marketing system. If you want to do all the hard work, and take the hundreds of hours to accomplish this, more power to you.

iii. Turn it over to me and let our system take the burden off your shoulders.

I will guide you through the process and work beside you at each step. I will show you how it integrates with your business to attract, convert, and retain customers.

Of these three options, the question that you will be asking yourself is, "How can I make this process easy for me and my business?"

I hope you're one of the people who take action when you see a good opportunity and are not the kind who sit on the fence and daydream. Those who act are the ones who earn respect, trust, and business in their community. Because you've read this far, I believe you are one of the uncommon few who takes action.

Schedule a consultation session with me and get started on your path to profit with your GDD Pixel Estate.

This call will help me understand your goals while we decide if working together is a good fit.

Thank you, and I look forward to speaking with you.

# Helpful Technology Resources

This is a partial list of technologies I use and recommend. For a complete list, please visit the book website PixelEstate.com/technologies. Please remember, the technologies I am recommending are my current opinion of my preferences at the time of the recommendation and may change or evolve over time. If you are using alternative technologies, that's your call. We all have our favorites. If you do become my private client, we will be using technologies of my choice because they are what our team is trained on, and we know how to support them.

- Inbound marketing and sales: HubSpot

- Cloud based customer experience automation: HubSpot

- CRM System: Email marketing and sales automation platform: HubSpot, Keap

- Website and sales funnel builder: ClickFunnels, WordPress, HubSpot

- Graphic design: Adobe Indesign, Illustrator, Photoshop, Microsoft Publisher

- Web Hosting: WP Engine

- Landing pages: Keap, HubSpot, ClickFunnels

- Website design CMS: HubSpot WordPress

- Membership sites: Customerhub, Imember360, Wordpress Wishlist

- Social media integration with Keap: Zapier, and Hubspot to Keap native integration

- PCI Compliance and ecommerce credit card processing: Authorize.net, Quickbooks Online

- Video editing : Adobe Premier

- Cloud Computing: Microsoft Office 365

- Online Calendar and Appointment Scheduling: Hubspot, Keap, Calendly

- Cloud file storage: Dropbox, Box, OneDrive, Adobe Creative Cloud

- Note-taking: Microsoft OneNote

- Mobile technology for the road: Latest Samsung phone with S-pen, Microsoft Surface, Microsoft Pen

- Project management and team collaboration: https://monday.com

- Email marketing (small budget or free tools): HubSpot, Keap

- Copywriting: No tune can replace a good copywriter. A machine can not do a Human's job. Skip the AI.

- Text messaging: Yetitext, Justcall, www.fixyourfunnel.com

- List research: www.srds.com (If you need help with list research please book time with me at www.meetparthiv.com)

- Data intelligence and data cleansing: Bulkmailer by Satori, Windowbook, Oracle for database programming

- Online data storage: MySQL

- Preferred programming language: PhP

- Online meeting: Zoom.com

- Reporting and analysis tools: Google Analytics, Infusionsoft Analytics, HubSpot CMS, Databox.com

With evolving technologies, this list becomes obsolete fast. If you are working to refresh or calibrate your Marketing Technologies Deck, I am here to help you understand your options and help you choose the most appropriate technology suite that is good for you. Just book a call with me at www.meetparthiv.com

# ABOUT
# PARTHIV SHAH

Parthiv Shah is president and founder of Elaunchers.com and a serial entrepreneur who has started five small businesses, including one internet start-up. He works on hundreds of different business models every year and contributes to their revenue model. For over 19 years, the direct marketing industry and thousands of case studies have been the fabric of his life. He has mailed over a billion pieces of direct mail throughout his career and brought in over fifteen million dollars in business to his company.

Parthiv has a passion for small business with a soft corner in his heart for start-ups and not-yet-started start-ups and contributes pro bono marketing consulting work for fellow entrepreneurs. Parthiv enjoys helping small businesses develop their value proposition and identify market segments most suitable to their strengths.

He has been an implementation craftsman and data scientist all his life and started his career in direct mail marketing in 1989. Shah learned many tricks of the trade while working with direct mail guru Matt Perrone from 1989 — 2002 at J Perrone Company in Hingham, MA. In 1999, Parthiv started a dot-com company, failed to make it a success, and went back to work for J Perrone company.

In 2002, he left J Perrone again to start in Pembroke, MA. Listlaunchers began as a mailing list company helping printers, mail houses, direct marketers, fundraisers, and ad agencies with their list research & data acquisition needs. It evolved into a full service online/offline marketing campaign implementation firm specializing in automated marketing.

In 2006, Parthiv sold Listlaunchers to an Indian InfoTech company and started eLaunchers.com. Elaunchers.com is a turnkey sales lead generation and marketing company that helps small, and no-so-small businesses and organizations compete against rivals who have deep pockets and large marketing budgets. The elaunchers.com team has developed a data-driven direct marketing process that integrates e-mail, direct mail, and web.

Since Shah enjoys helping small businesses grow, Elaunchers.com is a Done For You Implementation company helping small to mid-sized businesses experience a transformational marketing makeover within 48 hours to fifteen days. The entire game plays on Hubspot, WordPress, Infusionsoft, membership sites, SQL tables, PURL engine, and custom object-oriented programming.

Elaunchers.com has a global workforce with marketing and data experts in America, and API developers., Mobile App developers, and object-oriented programmers, and Web/CRM implementation specialists in other countries.

Shah has also taught marketing and e-business to MBA students at the University of Phoenix MBA School of Business.

Originally from India, he immigrated to the USA in 1990 and lived with his family in Randolph, Massachusetts, a little south of Boston. He resided in Boyds, Maryland, since 2014 when Elaunchers. com purchased the office space in Germantown, which is home to Elaunchers.com's corporate headquarters.

Shah has a bachelor's degree in sociology from Gujarat State University and an MBA in marketing from Bentley College.

**Book bonus:** To read additional books by Parthiv Shah's or to request an invitation to join his book club, please go to https://elaunchers.com/books.

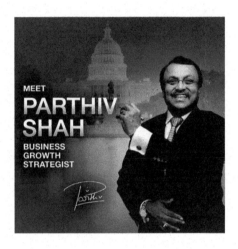

**Connect with Parthiv:**
Got questions? Want to talk to Parthiv? You can ask him questions at www.askparthiv.com or schedule a call with him at www.meetparthiv.com

# COULD I ASK YOU A SMALL FAVOR?

Thank you for reading my PIXEL ESTATE, How to build your Pixel Estate with Web Pages that Sell book! I know if you follow what I've written, you'll be on the right path to knowing what you need to automate your sales and marketing systems.

I have a tiny favor to ask. Would you be willing to leave a candid review for this book on Amazon?

Reviews are the best way to help other business owners and entrepreneurs solve problems by buying this book. I read all my reviews for helpful comments.

**If you have questions not addressed in my book, or you'd just like to share your feedback about my book, send me an email to <u>pshah@elaunchers.com</u>. I'd truly love to hear from you!**